The Skeptic's Guide™
to the
Global AIDS Crisis

Tough Questions
Direct Answers

Dale Hanson Bourke

Authentic
MEDIA

The Skeptic's Guide™ to the Global AIDS Crisis

Copyright © 2004 by Dale Hanson Bourke
This edition updated 2005

ISBN: 1-932805-20-6

09 08 07 06 05   6 5 4 3 2

Published by Authentic Media.
129 Mobilization Drive, Waynesboro, GA 30830 USA authenticusa@stl.org
and 9 Holdom Avenue, Bletchley, Milton Keynes, Bucks, MK1 1QR, UK
www.authenticbooks.org
To order additional copies or for our current catalog,
contact us at: 1-8MOREBOOKS • ordersusa@stl.org

Published in association with the literary agency of Alive Communication Inc.,
7680 Goddard Street #200, Colorado Springs, CO 80920.

Partial proceeds from the sale of this book will go to the
AIDS Orphan Bracelet Project
For more information about the project, visit www.aidsbracelets.org

Library of Congress Catalog-in-Publication data available.

Design: Ed Spivey Jr.

Printed in the United States of America

Acknowledgements

This book is really the result of the efforts of many people. Research was done by Kate Wilkinson and Chase Bourke, editing and review by Ann Claxton and Patton Dodd, proofing by Tom Richards, and Tyler Bourke helped his electronically-impaired mother find websites, files and her glasses. The design is the product of Ed Spivey's creativity and perseverance.

Many thanks to Volney James and Angela Duerksen of Authentic Publishing who shared the vision for this project from the start and invested in it personally and professionally. Thanks, too, to Tim Beals who got the project started and gave valuable insight into its direction. Rick Christian, my longtime agent, tended to the publishing details and understood that this was always a labor of love.

Many humanitarian groups contributed quotes, photos, publications, and data to this book as part of their ongoing commitment to the cause of HIV/AIDS. We have acknowledged them on the specific pages and hope the entire book offers a resource for them to use in their work.

Finally, thanks to all those who have been working on this cause for a very long time and whose tireless efforts have done so much to move us forward in understanding and compassion. May this be one more contribution to the much larger effort.

Contents

ACRONYMS

ABC	Abstain, Be Faithful, or Use Condoms
AIDS	Acquired Immunodeficiency Syndrome
ARV	Antiretroviral
CDC	Centers for Disease Control
CD4	Cluster Designation 4
CSW	Commercial Sex Worker
DNA	Deoxyribonucleic Acid
FBO	Faith-based Organization
FDA	Food and Drug Administration
FGM	Female Genital Mutilation
FSW	Female Sex Worker
HAART	Highly Active Antiretroviral Therapy
HIV	Human Immunodeficiency Virus
IAVI	International AIDS Vaccine Initiative
ILO	International Labor Organization
MTCT	Mother-to-Child Transmission
NGO	Non-governmental Organization
NIH	National Institutes of Health
PEPFAR	President's Emergency Plan for AIDS Relief
RNA	Ribonucleic Acid
STD	Sexually Transmitted Disease
UNAIDS	Joint United Nations Program on HIV/AIDS
UNICEF	United Nations Children's Fund
USAID	US Agency for International Development
WFP	World Food Program
WHO	World Health Organization
WTO	World Trade Organization

How much do you know about HIV/AIDS?

Test your knowledge with these True/False statements (answers on following page)

1. HIV/AIDS can be cured by new drug treatments if people can afford them.

2. In Russia, HIV infections are mostly spread by homosexual activity.

3. There are different strains of HIV, some more virulent than others.

4. Sub-Saharan Africa has so many cases of HIV/AIDS because of the large population.

5. By 2010 India will have more people infected by HIV/AIDS than any other country in the world if trends continue.

6. More men than women are infected with HIV/AIDS worldwide.

7. Pregnant women who are HIV positive almost always have babies who are infected.

8. There are hundreds of thousands of Americans living with HIV/AIDS.

9. Men who are circumcised are more likely to be infected with HIV and to spread it to others.

10. A person who has AIDS can be granted asylum in the US on grounds of persecution.

Quiz Answers

1. FALSE. There is no cure for HIV/AIDS, but there are treatments. See page 33.

2. FALSE. Russia has a rapidly growing rate of HIV/AIDS infection primarily due to IV drug use. See page 65.

3. TRUE. Researchers believe there are at least three different strains with multiple sub-strains, some more virulent than others. See page 15.

4. FALSE. Sub-Sahara is home to about 10 percent of the world's population but two-thirds of all people living with HIV. See page 13.

5. TRUE. There are approximately 5.1 million people infected in India today. See page 21.

6. FALSE. There are about an equal number of men and women infected worldwide, with more women than men infected in Africa. See page 22.

7. FALSE. Mother-to-child-transmission averages 30 percent but in developed countries has been reduced to a very low rate. See page 15.

8. TRUE. At the end of 2003, more than 700,000 Americans were living with HIV or AIDS. See chart on page 9.

9. FALSE. Some studies indicate that circumcision helps reduce infection and transmission. See page 27.

10. TRUE. Asylum can be granted to individuals who can prove that their HIV/AIDS status is causing them to be persecuted in their country. See page 71.

About the Author

Dale Hanson Bourke is an award-winning writer and a dedicated humanitarian. She is the author of five books, has written a weekly syndicated newspaper column, served as editor and publisher of several magazines, and has traveled extensively in developing countries.

She has also served on the board of directors of World Vision US and World Vision International, and currently serves on the board of International Justice Mission and Opportunity International. She is the founder of the AIDS Orphan Bracelet Project.

Dale lives with her husband and two sons near Washington, DC.

INTRODUCTION

I am not an AIDS expert. Quite the opposite, in fact. I am an ordinary woman who had heard enough about AIDS to know it was a big problem, but not enough to worry about it. I had the good old American belief that if I really needed to know something about AIDS, I'd get an official notice in the mail or the newspapers would carry big headlines.

No notice came, and the headlines only confused me. AIDS stories carried incomprehensible statistics and arguments over drugs, treatments, politics, and issues I had neither the time nor the inclination to explore. I figured I'd let everyone fight it out and get back to me when they had settled the real issues. After all, if things were so bad, why did everyone waste time bickering?

Like many people, I had become a skeptic about AIDS. The panic in the US in the early 1990s had given way to moderation and the understanding that people with AIDS were not a serious threat to me or my children. And besides, Magic Johnson was alive and well, wasn't he? Maybe it had just been a passing phase.

But unlike most people, I had the opportunity to travel to Africa and Asia. There I was confronted with the irrefutable evidence that I—and many people like me—was missing something.

In Africa I saw roadside stands with wooden coffins being sold as quickly as they could be made. In Asia I visited a home for sick and orphaned children whose mothers were prostitutes who had died of AIDS. In one country, I met a wrinkled and stooped-over woman who, barely able to walk, had to care for ten children, including an infant. Through a translator, she explained that these were her grandchildren, the survivors of her own sons and daughters, all of whom had died of AIDS. "Pray for me that I will live long enough to

FACT:

AIDS is the first epidemic of a *new* disease since the 1400s.

raise these children," she implored, her eyes filled with tears.

It didn't take long for these encounters to motivate me to action. But what could I do? It seemed like there was an immense gap between what I knew and what it would take to really help someone.

I looked for a basic book that would help me understand the situation. I found some good material, but most of it raised more questions. As I became more interested in the topic, I began to ask other people what they knew. Soon I realized that when it comes to HIV/AIDS, most of us have a pretty steep learning curve.

This book grows out of the questions I and many others have asked about HIV and AIDS. The answers come from interviews, other books, and official statistics provided by the World Health Organization and the United Nations. I try to deliver the most basic facts, explaining medical and political issues in everyday language.

If you are an expert, this book will seem simplistic. If you have a strong point of view on one or more of the issues surrounding AIDS, you will probably find that I have stated your view right alongside an opposing point of view. I have tried hard to represent controversies so that readers can not only decide what they believe but also understand how those who believe differently have reached their conclusions.

While I have asked a variety of people to review these materials, I may not have represented every point of view accurately. Feel free to send in your thoughts and we will try to get it right in the next edition.

And, of course, this book cannot help but talk about sex, although it is mostly in clinical terms. There is simply no way to discuss HIV/AIDS without acknowledging the primary way it is spread.

As you read, remember that things change

almost daily in the world of AIDS. Theories shift as facts are tested and proven or disproved. Certain points of view pick up baggage as they become associated with certain organizations or causes. Legal challenges prevail and governments change policies. Statistical projections are recalculated and appear to change the facts.

AIDS is not just a medical issue. It is a political, legal, religious, economic, cultural, and historic issue. It is a dynamic, evolving field with a highly complex combination of variables. To try to simplify these and freeze them at one point in time is to accept that as soon as this book is printed it will begin to be out of date.

Thus, this is simply a start. It is a way to begin a conversation about a very important topic. It is meant to help you feel you know enough to not be frustrated.

From here, you can read more books, consider the editorials, listen to experts. Tell someone else, start a study group, pray. By reading this book, you take a step toward understanding. Just as education is the first step in preventing the spread of AIDS, so it is also the first step in combating the type of skepticism that spreads complacency.

—*Dale Hanson Bourke*

FACT:

SIDA is the acronym for AIDS in French, Spanish and other romance languages.

Eleven-year-old Dejene holds photos of his parents who died of AIDS.

THE BASICS

While interviewing a variety of people from different walks of life, similar questions arose about HIV/AIDS. Following are some of the basic questions and answers. Almost all of these are discussed in more detail later, but if you're looking for a quick overview, this section is for you.

Just how bad is the international AIDS crisis?

■ AIDS is the biggest public health problem the world has ever faced. It has already surpassed the bubonic plague, which wiped out twenty-five million people—one quarter of Europe's population at the time. An estimated three million people die each year from AIDS, a death toll that has been compared to twenty fully loaded 747s crashing every single day for a year.

AIDS has now spread to every country in the world. In most cases, the rate of infection and death is increasing rapidly. Although the highest number of infected people live in Africa, countries in Asia are showing a rapid rate of growth. Reported AIDS cases are rising so swiftly in China and India that they could eventually eclipse the numbers in Africa.

AIDS typically infects people in the prime of life, depriving children of their parents, and communities of their most productive workers. In some countries more than one-third of the population is infected, effectively wiping out an entire generation.

Since many people are HIV positive for years without showing symptoms, no one really knows the magnitude of the problem. Most people in poorer countries are never tested, and many that die of AIDS-related infections are officially listed as succumbing to tuberculosis or malaria in order to keep their families from being stigmatized.

Most estimates show the rate of infection and death growing at a high rate at least until 2010, even with aggressive worldwide interventions. Experts from various disciplines agree that the problems associated with AIDS will dominate the entire twenty-first century.

What is the difference between an epidemic and a pandemic?

■ An epidemic is an illness that occurs and spreads to many more people than would be statistically expected during a point in time. A pandemic is an epidemic that occurs over a large geographic area, usually worldwide.

What's with all the initials? What do they mean?

■ HIV stands for human immunodeficiency virus. Human means it affects men, women and children. Immunodeficiency refers to a decline in the body's natural ability to fight infection. Virus means it is a small, infectious organism that reproduces inside a person. AIDS stands for acquired immunodeficiency syndrome. Acquired means it is not genetic. Immunodeficiency, as with HIV, means that the immune system has become very weak or ineffective. Syndrome refers to a group of symptoms that occur together and characterize a disease.

Another series of initials associated with HIV/AIDS is ARV, which stands for antiretroviral drugs. ARVs offer treatment, but not a cure. They help a person fight the virus and improve the ability to resist other infections. ARVs reduce the rate of replication of retroviruses such as HIV. Retroviruses are a particular type of virus that store their genetic information on an RNA molecule instead of a DNA molecule, part of the reason this disease is different from others and more difficult to tackle.

A more detailed list of initials and their meanings appears on page vi.

What's the difference between HIV and AIDS?

■ AIDS and HIV are not the same thing. A person may be infected with HIV for many years before developing AIDS, which is considered to be the last stage of the illness resulting from the HIV virus.

A person with HIV may not show any major symptoms of infection. Or, there may be flu-like symptoms in the first month or two, such as fever, headaches, or swollen glands. During this period, the person may not test positive for HIV but is able to transmit the disease.

After this initial phase, the person may be free of symptoms for many years. During this time, the virus is invading and attacking a person's CD4 cells, often known as T-cells. T-cells are the body's

primary defense against viruses and bacteria. A person with a high T-cell count is waging a war on an internal infection. But when HIV begins to take over, T-cells are slowly defeated and destroyed. A healthy person has a T-cell count of 500–1500. According to the Centers for Disease Control (CDC), when a person with HIV has a T-cell count at or below 200, the person is considered to have AIDS—the most severe manifestation of HIV.

With such a low T-cell count, a person is susceptible to other infections which the body might ordinarily be able to fight. In developing countries, someone with a suppressed immune system can readily contract tuberculosis, malaria, hepatitis, or other diseases commonly occurring in the environment. At that point, a person with AIDS can become a carrier of other highly communicable diseases, creating additional health risks for other people.

How are HIV and AIDS diagnosed?

■ A blood test is required to accurately diagnose HIV, although it may not show up until six months after infection. AIDS can be diagnosed either through measuring the T-cell count or when a number of opportunistic infections or cancers become present in a person with HIV. A person with AIDS may live for a few years or succumb quickly to another disease.

How are HIV and AIDS treated?

■ Antiretroviral drugs may be used with a person who has HIV or AIDS, and have been effective in treating both.

In the US, everyone panicked when AIDS was first reported, but now things don't seem so bad. Isn't it possible that we are overstating the problem?

■ When the first cases of AIDS were reported in the US, some of the best medical minds went to work on the problem. The blood supply was tested and purged of potentially infected blood. "At-risk" populations were urged to have HIV tests. The fact that the gay community was hardest hit also meant that a group of people who were generally well educated and well resourced brought considerable attention to the problem. With high visibility, most people in the US quickly learned about AIDS and how it was transmitted.

Although nearly 500,000 individuals have died of AIDS in the US, the rate of infection has decreased by 70 percent since 1994. Those who are HIV positive have also benefited from drug therapies that have prolonged their lives.

Elsewhere, the situation is much worse. In poor countries, many people still do not know about the risk of AIDS. When people in impoverished villages are infected, they are often already in bad health and malnourished, so their bodies have difficulty fighting the disease. Inefficient health care systems have helped spread the infection through tainted blood supplies and non-ster-

Adults and children estimated to be living with HIV/AIDS, end 2004

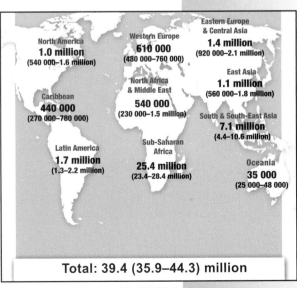

North America
1.0 million
(540 000–1.6 million)

Western Europe
610 000
(480 000–760 000)

Eastern Europe & Central Asia
1.4 million
(920 000–2.1 million)

North Africa & Middle East
540 000
(230 000–1.5 million)

East Asia
1.1 million
(560 000–1.8 million)

Caribbean
440 000
(270 000–780 000)

South & South-East Asia
7.1 million
(4.4–10.6 million)

Latin America
1.7 million
(1.3–2.2 million)

Sub-Saharan Africa
25.4 million
(23.4–28.4 million)

Oceania
35 000
(25 000–48 000)

Total: 39.4 (35.9–44.3) million

UNAIDS/WHO

ile instruments and facilities. Lack of understanding has also led to myths and denial, which has only helped spread the disease. Many governments lack the will to admit the problem exists, and even when they do, they have limited resources to address it. Many countries still have few testing facilities.

If anything, most experts believe the AIDS problem is understated and underreported.

What about Magic Johnson? Wasn't he diagnosed with AIDS, but is still fine?

■ Magic Johnson, the famous basketball star, disclosed in 1991 that he was HIV positive, but he had not developed AIDS. The virus was discovered at a very early stage, and as an athlete in top condition, Johnson's immune system was probably very strong. He was able to receive the best medical care and was immediately placed on a regimen of drug treatments. (See the discussion of drug treatments on page 33). Because of this treatment, the HIV virus has remained at a very low level.

Johnson's example illustrates how drug treatments can not only prolong the life of someone who is HIV positive but can offer the chance for a relatively normal and active life. Many public health officials point out that if similar drug treatments are available and people do not believe that being HIV positive is a death sentence, the environment will be conducive to wider HIV testing. Such a reduced stigma could combat the pandemic in many ways, not least of which is reducing the transmission of the virus from mothers to their babies.

> " The world cannot underestimate the threat of AIDS, but it would be equally wrong to fall into despair."
>
> **Kofi Annan**
> **Secretary-General of the UN**

Mauritania was one of the African countries taking a lead in AIDS prevention. This billboard appeared in 1995.

Dale Hanson Bourke

If most cases occur overseas, why would the US government declare the HIV/AIDS pandemic a threat to national security?

- In 2000, the US government declared the growing HIV/AIDS pandemic a threat to national security. One reason for doing so has to do with the fact that our world is shrinking and is highly interconnected. The US is one day's travel away from many countries.

In addition, in some countries, AIDS is primarily wiping out the young adult population, leaving only children and the elderly behind. The average age in many African countries is declining rapidly. This is destabilizing socially, economically, and politically. Over the next decade, this trend will continue, potentially derailing the progress these countries have made during the last century.

Children in these countries will grow up in a society that has moved backwards in terms of education, healthcare, agriculture, and other development indicators. They will enter adulthood with our children, being closely connected through travel and communication, but having backgrounds of immense poverty and hardship. It is understandable that such conditions could lead to radical leadership. Senator Bill Frist has said that children growing up in the shadow of AIDS constitute "a pool of recruits for terrorists."

Where did AIDS come from?

- AIDS was first clinically identified in 1983, but it is believed to have existed for many years before that. The virus closest to it is simian immunodeficiency virus, a disease found in monkeys in equatorial Africa. Some believe that the virus jumped from animals to humans when infected "bush meat"—the meat of monkeys—was eaten, a common practice in that region.

Others have hypothesized that a polio vaccine used in the 1950s was cultivated on monkeys in Africa and may have transmitted a strain of the virus to humans, especially those whose immune systems were compromised through poor nutrition and other diseases. This theory is controversial and tends to fuel conspiracy theories. Scientists do know that other viruses jump from animals to humans, including some forms of influenza and the disease known as SARS.

For many years in Africa, there was a mysterious disease called "Slims." Infected people tended to lose weight and become very thin. (Many in Africa still use this term to refer to those with AIDS.) Some believe that HIV/AIDS may have existed in Africa for decades before it was clinically identified, providing the virus with the opportunity to become more virulent as it mutated and found a way to efficiently infect humans. How it first jumped to humans may never be known, but it probably happened decades ago.

What is UNAIDS?

■ The United Nations Program on HIV/AIDS (UNAIDS) is a joint program of nine organizations, including: the United Nations Children's Fund (UNICEF); the World Food Program; the United Nations Development Program (UNDP); the International Labor Organization (ILO); the United Nations Population Fund (UNFPA); the World Health Organization (WHO); the United Nations Educational, Scientific and Cultural Organization (UNESCO); the World Bank; and the United Nations Office on Drugs and Crime (UNODC).

The program's purpose is to lead, strengthen, and support an expanded response aimed at preventing transmission of HIV, providing care and support, reducing the vulnerability of individuals and communities to HIV/AIDS, and alleviating the impact of the epidemic. UNAIDS provides the information most often used when talking about the pandemic and plays a central role in coordinating responses. The UNAIDS website, www.unaids.org, is one of the best places for reliable information about AIDS.

What is meant by sub-Saharan Africa, and why is AIDS so bad there?

■ Sub-Saharan Africa is the part of Africa south of the Sahara Desert. Although this is the largest part of Africa geographically, it tends to be sparsely populated except in major cities. Sub-Saharan Africa is usually considered to include forty-seven countries, many of which are among the poorest in the world. While it is home to only 10 percent

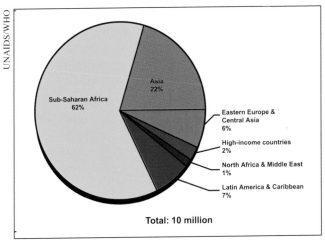

UNAIDS/WHO

Total: 10 million

Young people (15-24 years old) living with HIV, by region, end 2003.

of the world's population, nearly 70 percent of those infected with HIV/AIDS live there, according to UNAIDS.

AIDS is believed to have started in this region. Countries here typically have poor public health facilities and fragmented communication systems, and many have unstable governments.

Because of these circumstances and the fact that diseases such as malaria, tuberculosis, and dysentery had been claiming lives in such great numbers for so many years, it is possible AIDS was not even noticed at first. The biggest difference between AIDS and the other epidemics was that AIDS was claiming the lives of more adults than children.

The rate of infection continues to grow in most countries in this region because there are still many people who have not been educated about the disease and how it spreads. This region of Africa is also believed to have the most virulent strain of AIDS.

Isn't AIDS mostly a homosexual disease?

■ While AIDS in the US has had its highest incidence in the gay community, internationally, HIV is primarily transmitted through heterosexual sex, intravenous drug use, transmission from infected mothers to their babies, and infection through the blood supply. The virus does not exist for long outside of the body so early fears about contracting the virus through casual contact have been laid to rest. Worldwide, it is not primarily a disease of homosexuals. More women than men are infected in Africa, and many are infected by their husbands.

HIV is transmitted through contact with blood, semen, vaginal, or amniotic fluid and breast milk. Although the virus is found in saliva, tears, and perspiration, the concentration is generally too low for transmission. Unless a person has a cut or tear in the skin, he or she cannot be infected by dealing with human waste of those infected. Neither can a person be infected by sharing utensils with an infected person, swimming or bathing in the same water, being bitten by an insect, or being coughed or sneezed on, according to the Centers for Disease Control (CDC).

> **"AIDS is the greatest weapon of mass destruction on earth."**
> **Colin Powell**
> **Secretary of State**

Although HIV/AIDS is, itself, often a sexually transmitted disease (STD), the risk of transmitting or contracting the disease is increased by the presence of another STD in either partner.

Do infected mothers always pass the virus to their babies?

■ Not necessarily. Women may pass the virus to their babies in three different ways: during pregnancy through the placenta; during childbirth; and through breast milk. Without treatment, between 15 to 30 percent of babies born to HIV-positive mothers are infected. Caesarian deliveries reduce this to some degree.

Mother-to-child transmission (MTCT) is an area of great interest since it is now known that relatively simple drug interventions seem to be able to prevent the infection of an infant whose mother is HIV positive. If there is a story of hope in the middle of the crisis, it is in the growing movement to help pregnant women who are HIV positive bear children who are free of the virus. In developed countries, such interventions have helped reduce the rate of transmission to a very small percentage.

Because breastfeeding also transmits the virus, and since so many poor women have no safe alternative for feeding their babies, transmission to infants continues. Still, since infants carry their mother's antibodies for at least the first year, a baby may test positive in the early months but be free of HIV by the age of two.

Are there different types of viruses?

■ Yes. Experts believe there are at least three distinct strains of the virus, with as many as eleven subtypes. The virus also appears to be very adaptable and seems to mutate. Certain strains or subtypes seem to dominate in different regions,

FACT:

AIDS has killed millions of people in China, many of whom were infected by donating blood (using non-sterile needles) in order to provide income for their poor families.

depending on the primary source of transmission and other factors. As testing methods improve, researchers are finding that strains can dominate a region, and then another strain can overtake rapidly, requiring different methods of treatment.

What's all the controversy about making drugs available to treat AIDS?

■ Antiretroviral drugs have been widely available in the US for more than ten years and have significantly decreased symptoms and prolonged the lives of those who are HIV positive. The drug therapies have greatly improved. Treatments known as HAART—highly active antiretroviral therapies—have not only shown marked improvement in suppressing symptoms but have also been shown to suppress the virus itself, possibly making an individual less prone to infect others. This is especially true in reducing transmission from HIV positive women to their babies.

Drug therapies produced in the US and Europe are expensive but the same drugs are being manufactured much less expensively in other countries. The main cost associated with producing drugs has to do with patents held by drug companies. There has been pressure, especially on Western drug companies, to allow the drugs to be produced without the patent fee for use in developing countries. Meanwhile, generic drugs are being produced in violation of patents. But those drugs cannot be used in US-funded programs unless they have passed FDA testing.

The cost of drugs has dropped considerably over the past year, down to about a dollar a day in many cases. The Clinton Foundation has also been involved in negotiating lower prices for bulk distribution, which has brought the cost of some therapies down as low as $140 per year.

Treatment with these drugs does require some medical oversight. That makes treatment difficult for many people in developing countries who simply don't have ready access to clinics or doctors. In addition, because there are various strains of the virus, it is important to find the right combination or dosage of drugs to match the nature of the infection. And in order for treatment to be effective, it must continue throughout the lifetime of infected individuals. But in a recent trial in Uganda, participants demonstrated a 97 percent compliance rate, helping show that those in developing countries can use drugs effectively.

Although the cost of drugs has been reduced to less than a dollar a day for those in developing countries, this is still an unimaginable expense for the poor. And the drugs themselves are only part of the cost of the treatment. As drug therapies become more widely available, public health officers and politicians are working to provide some type of protocol so that the drugs will not just go to the rich, but will be available to those who can be helped most, such as pregnant women.

Why isn't the media reporting more about the issue?

■ HIV/AIDS infection rates are generally reported each year when UNAIDS and WHO issue their annual reports. But otherwise, AIDS is no longer news. It is an ongoing crisis that has been around for twenty years and will be around for at least another twenty. Sadly, most reporting is done when there is controversy.

Most infections and deaths continue to occur in Africa, and some critics note the dearth of any reporting on Africa. Tuberculosis and malaria have been killing millions of people in African countries for years, but a few cases of West Nile virus in the US typically get far more coverage.

FACT:

By 2010, it is estimated that there will be 25 million AIDS orphans in the world.

Pharmaceutical worker in Bangkok sorts AIDS antiretroviral drugs.

HEALTH ISSUES

The various medical and public health issues associated with HIV/AIDS are complex and dynamic. These answers offer basic explanations of many questions people have asked about health-related issues.

It seems that there has been controversy over AIDS from the beginning. Wasn't there even disagreement over who discovered the virus?

■ There has been controversy, in part because AIDS is both new and also so deadly. The stakes are high and the learning curve is steep. Not only are researchers and medical doctors involved, but also politicians, social workers, religious leaders, lawyers, and others, and everyone is claiming some part of the debate.

Evidence of the disease was seen in various countries by the late 1970s. Doctors began to see an increasing number of patients with an unusual strain of pneumonia and rare cancers. Some noticed that it appeared most often in gay men and began to call it Gay-Related Immune Deficiency Syndrome or GRID. In 1983, the human immunodeficiency virus was first isolated by Luc Montagnier at the French Institut Pasteur. It was called lymphadenopathy-associated virus (LAV). Then, in the US, Dr. Robert Gallo of the National Cancer Institute discovered something he called HTLV-3. At some point the research community realized that the two had discovered the same virus, and in 1986 it was renamed HIV.

Because there was a belief that a vaccine would soon be developed, resulting in a lucrative patent, the US and France fought over who had discovered the virus first and who would control the rights.

Eventually the French researcher was deemed to have discovered the virus, although no vaccine has been developed.

All the statistics are confusing. Haven't the total numbers actually gone down?

■ Measuring the rate of infection and even death in a pandemic is daunting, but this is especially true with AIDS. As mentioned earlier, most people in developing countries who are HIV positive don't even know they are infected. Through lack of understanding or desire to avoid stigma, AIDS deaths in many countries are often attributed to tuberculosis or another disease. Many times there are no official records. And, of course, many of those with immune systems compromised by AIDS actually do succumb to other diseases. Some countries have also tried to hide their AIDS problem, fearing that it would hurt tourism or make the country seem vulnerable.

Because of all those factors, numbers relating to AIDS are almost always stated as estimates and in ranges, and various methods are used to continue to refine the numbers.

Between 2002 and 2003, the groups involved in developing estimates agreed on more accurate ways to arrive at their figures. The numbers of those infected released in 2003 appeared to be lower than the previous year, but they were simply a revised estimate. The rate of infection has not decreased; the way of stating it has just become more refined.

Another factor to remember is that in some countries the infection rate appears to be declining when, in fact, the rate of deaths is growing faster than the infection rate. In other words, people are no longer counted as infected when they become part of the mortality statistics.

66

We have a saying in Uganda:'One plus one soon makes a bundle.' We understand that each person makes a difference. We know that each person in your country can make a difference too."

Robinah Bobirye
Director of
HIV/AIDS
Initiative,
Opportunity
International

Why do some statistics use the "incidence" of HIV/AIDS while others discuss "prevalence"? Aren't they the same thing?

■ No. Incidence is used to measure the actual number of new infections. If you look at the incidence of infections year to year, you can see if the epidemic is increasing. Annual incidence figures subtract one year's numbers from the previous year's.

Prevalence measures the percentage of people in the total population infected at a given point in time. When related to HIV/AIDS, prevalence is always given as a percentage. A country with a large population may have a very high incidence rate but a small prevalence rate. Conversely, a country with a small population might have the same incidence rate as another country but a much higher prevalence rate.

In India, 5.1 million people are estimated to be infected with HIV. That's higher than any country other than South Africa. But because of its large population, the prevalence of HIV/AIDS in India is low. In Botswana, where the prevalence rate is more than 35 percent, the number of people living with HIV/AIDS is much less, but the effects of having more than a third of the population infected are devastating.

Some researchers believe that when the prevalence rate reaches 5 percent, the infection "takes off" in the total population and begins to increase at a higher rate throughout the country.

How is life expectancy measured?

■ Life expectancy is the level of mortality in a population at a particular time. It is measured in years and basically gives the average age at which a person in that population could expect to die.

FACT:

In African countries, studies estimate that between 19 percent and 53 percent of all government health employee deaths are caused by AIDS.

Life expectancy is viewed as a health indicator and is a way to view the overall well-being of a population. Infant mortality rates also affect life expectancy measures. In many African countries, life expectancy has dropped considerably because such a large number of people have died at a relatively early age.

Is it true that it is easier for a woman to be infected through sex than for a man?

■ According to the most recent UNAIDS report, women in Africa are more likely to be infected than men. The rate varies by country, but is as high as 65 percent of the infections in Kenya. Internationally, the rate of infection is about equal between men and women.

A woman is more likely to be infected by her partner because she is more likely to harbor infected fluids in her body, where they have more opportunity to enter her bloodstream. Also girls are often married or sexually initiated in adolescence in some societies, and it is thought that a young girl is physically smaller and more vulnerable to tears and abrasions, therefore more susceptible to infections. The practice of female circumcision, also called female genital mutilation (FGM), makes a woman more likely to have complications, which also increases her tendency to be infected.

It is also true that women in many cultures are more vulnerable to infection because of their low status in society and in the family as well as a sexual double standard which exposes them to many risk factors. Sex is a taboo subject in many countries, and most youth do not receive any kind of sex education in the family or in school. Deeply ingrained gender roles require that girls, especially, are expected to be sexually naïve, inexperienced, and submissive, while virility for men means multiple partners.

"
Columbus had a strong feeling but didn't know how far it was to land. It's the same with AIDS vaccines."

Emilio Emini
Vice President and chief of vaccine development at The International AIDS Vaccine Initiative (IAVI)
Quoted in *Business Week*, July 2004

A woman in many societies is expected to be submissive to her partner and does not feel entitled or might be afraid to suggest the use of condoms, even if she suspects he has had other partners. Arranged marriages are common in developing countries and age disparity is also common since the girl's family seeks a husband who is already well established in an occupation, while the man is seeking a young girl more likely to be a virgin and uninfected.

Sadly, poverty is a major pressure on girls and women, who often resort to exchanging sex for cash or gifts such as educational fees and even food.

Finally, rape is an all-too-common occurrence in many poor countries. In some African countries, there is a widespread belief that having sex with a virgin will cure AIDS. This myth has contributed to an alarming increase in the rape of young women and girls.

Speaking to the International AIDS Conference in Bangkok in July 2004, Stephen Lewis, the UN Special Envoy for HIV/AIDS in Africa, called for governments to enact and enforce laws against rape, sexual violence, discrimination, loss of property rights, and other situations that hurt women. He also asked for laws to raise the legal marriage age.

FACT:

The ILO projects that the labor force in 38 countries will be between 5 percent and 35 percent smaller by 2020 because of AIDS.

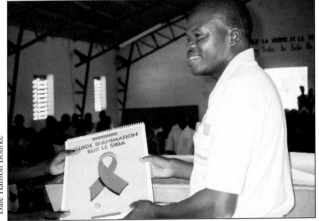

Dale Hanson Bourke

Seminarians in Burkina Faso receive training on AIDS as part of their preparation for becoming ministers.

Why are sexually transmitted diseases (STDs) a factor in HIV/AIDS transmission?

■ Many STDs cause ulcers, sores, or other breaks in the skin, which make HIV infection easier to transmit into the bloodstream. In addition, doctors believe that when a person's immune system is already fighting another STD infection, the very cells the HIV infection are seeking to invade are concentrated and therefore more easily infected in large numbers.

What are people referring to when they talk about the ABCs of AIDS?

■ ABC refers to three most effective behaviors people can choose to avoid or reduce the risk of sexually transmitted diseases, including HIV. A is for abstinence, B is for "be faithful," and C is for the use of condoms. This approach has been used in Uganda and elsewhere as part of a campaign that has reduced the rate of infection significantly.

In 1986, Uganda's President Museveni launched a program to raise awareness and reverse the spread of HIV/AIDS in his country. A major part of the program was education about prevention. In an effort to help spread the message in a simple way, it was promoted as the ABCs, in that order of priority. Another phrase associated with the effort was "Zero Grazing," referring to the practice of keeping cattle within their boundaries and out of neighbor's fields, and applied in this case to encourage fidelity.

Dr. Edward Green, a Harvard medical anthropologist who studied the initiative, has written about it in his book, *Rethinking AIDS Prevention* (Praeger, 2003). He observes that the primary emphasis was the push for marital faithfulness,

> **Among the many myths spawned by the global AIDS crisis, the belief that there is 'nothing we can do' is one of the most destructive."**
> **From *Global AIDS: Myths and Facts* (South End Press, 2003) Alexander Irwin, Joyce Millen and Dorothy Fallows**

since in Ugandan culture men often had several sexual partners, a practice widely accepted even by faith leaders.

So why is there so much controversy associated with this position?

■ According to Dr. Green's findings, monogamy, partner reduction, and abstinence were stronger factors in prevention in Uganda than the use of condoms. This was due to many reasons, including the fact that condoms were not widely available, especially early in the effort. Ugandan men resisted using condoms and were, therefore, inconsistent in their usage when they were available. And partner faithfulness became part of a cultural movement that changed the way Ugandan society viewed sexual experience, especially among young people.

Dr. Green's premise was widely accepted by faith communities and was promoted by the Bush administration. It was a priority in the prevention goals of the president's AIDS initiative. Some faith-based organizations resisted promoting the use of condoms, placing more emphasis on abstinence and fidelity. Thus, abstinence programs became associated with what some considered a conservative agenda.

Some critics felt that this emphasis on abstinence was unrealistic, especially for women and girls who had little power to resist the advances of men in their culture. Others believed that funding programs that promoted abstinence more than condom use was pushing an American point of view.

However, as Dr. Green's findings show, all prevention programs should include abstinence and fidelity components. The controversy has to do with how much emphasis is given to particular components and how efficacy is measured.

FACT:

Eastern Europe and Central Asia have the fastest growing HIV/AIDS epidemic, fueled largely by injection drug use.

What are microbicides?

■ Microbicides are usually gels or foams that can be used to destroy bacteria or viruses. They are being researched as a possible method for protecting women from contracting HIV. Because it has been difficult to get men in many cultures to use condoms consistently, attention is being placed on finding ways for women to protect themselves, especially by using something that is not obvious to their partner. Some researchers even believe that a microbicide could be developed that would dramatically reduce the chance of HIV infection while at the same time allowing a woman to become pregnant. Since women in many countries place a high value on fertility, such a method would be very popular.

Why do some groups oppose the use of condoms?

■ There are organizations that do not promote the use of condoms at all, while other groups simply promote certain types of prevention more than condom usage. Some religious organizations believe that condom use encourages promiscuity or early sexual activity. Others oppose all methods of birth control, including condoms. Some feel that condoms are undependable and should not be encouraged over abstinence. Others point out that the cost of condoms is too great of a burden on the poor, and it is not realistic to believe they will be used regularly.

Do condoms really stop the transmission of sexually transmitted diseases?

■ There have been some groups who have asserted that condoms do not stop STDs. It's true that condoms made of natural materials as opposed to latex or polyurethane have pores that may allow transmission of such microbes. But according to the CDC, latex or polyurethane condoms, when used correctly and continuously, do prevent the transmission of HIV and other STDs.

However, these studies have been done in laboratories. Condoms used in real life are susceptible to being reduced in efficacy by heat, sunlight, ozone, lubricants, tears, and improper usage. Most men prefer not to use condoms because they believe condoms reduce pleasure. Some women in developing countries don't like condoms because they block their ability to become pregnant. And, as previously mentioned, condoms are expensive for poor people and must be re-supplied, another challenge for those living outside major cities.

What is meant by "dry sex"?

■ Some men, especially in Africa, prefer to have sex with a woman whose vagina is not lubricated, thereby creating more friction. Women often use herbs or other products to accomplish this, not knowing that it creates more risk of HIV infection because the practice can result in more tears in the woman's vaginal area. This also creates additional friction and can tear a condom if used.

Does circumcision prevent HIV infection and transmission?

■ Some studies seem to indicate that men who are circumcised are less likely to become infected or pass on an infection. But the studies done so far have not been able to rule out other possible factors, so more are underway.

Public health officials first noticed that there was a different rate of infection between Muslim men, who are generally circumcised, and men of other backgrounds. Ruling out certain religious practices seemed to continue to show a correlation, and there are some health professionals who believe the lack of foreskin prevents the harboring of disease. There is also some evidence that the foreskin itself contains certain types of cells that are more susceptible to being infected by the virus.

What is female circumcision?

■ What is sometimes called female circumcision is more widely known as female genital mutilation (FGM) and is condemned by both the World Health Organization and human rights groups. Those who practice it sometimes consider it a coming of age ritual, although it is practiced on girls as young as infants and seems to be most prevalent among girls between the ages of four and eight.

FGM removes part of the female genitalia and is often performed with an unsterilized knife. Besides being painful, the practice often leaves young women with chronic infection problems in both their urinary and reproductive tracts. It can result in incontinence as well as complications in childbirth. The practice itself, as well as the complications associated with it, are considered to further expose girls to HIV infection.

FGM is primarily practiced in certain African countries. It is practiced by members of all religions, although no religion officially requires it, according to the WHO.

Is homosexuality a factor worldwide, or mostly in Western countries?

■ Homosexuality does exist in other parts of the world, but probably not to the extent that it does in more wealthy, developed countries. The practice is highly stigmatized in Africa, Asia, and Latin America and is illegal in eighty-four countries. Worldwide, UNAIDS estimates that HIV infections from men to men account for 5–10 percent of all infections. Because relationships between men are far more hidden in developing countries, it is particularly difficult to find effective ways to teach AIDS prevention to men in this group.

Why don't more people get tested so they know if they are carrying the virus?

■ There are few testing facilities in many poor countries. Even if a facility is available, obtaining tests can be costly and difficult. Asking to be tested means you are admitting you have engaged in risky behavior. (One of the ways to encourage testing is for leaders and famous individuals to be tested.) Few testing facilities in developing countries can comply with the WHO testing guidelines, and until recently, it often took days for the results, requiring a return visit.

Finally, many public health officials point out that until there is treatment available, few people will really seek testing. If finding out you are infected is not a death sentence, there is a higher probability that there will be more voluntary testing.

What are the World Health Organization guidelines for HIV testing?

■ UNAIDS and the World Health Organization have developed a policy on testing that is intended to encourage the practice, especially among those who are in countries with a high incidence of HIV. The policy can be summarized as the "Three Cs": Testing must be **confidential**; testing must be accompanied by **counseling**; and testing must be conducted with informed **consent**.

While UNAIDS/WHO support mandatory screening of blood or organ donors and of the blood itself, they do not support mandatory testing of

FACT:

Sexually transmitted infections increase the risk of HIV transmission by at least two to five times.

individuals on the grounds of public health facilities. They believe that voluntary testing is more likely to result in behavior change.

What are the symptoms of HIV infection?

■ A person who has been infected with HIV may experience swollen glands, fever, nausea, fatigue, and overall aches. These symptoms are often mistaken for the "flu" and will eventually subside. After that a person may have no symptoms for years and appear very healthy, even though he or she is infectious. When a person develops AIDS, there is typically weight loss, sores and rashes, lack of energy, fever, swollen glands, chronic diarrhea, and such opportunistic infections as thrush.

How close are scientists to finding a vaccine for the virus?

■ Some of the best scientific minds are working on developing a vaccine, but most admit it is an extremely difficult challenge. Some even fear that they may never find prevention or a cure.

There are a number of reasons for their pessimism. The nature of the virus itself makes it hard to attack without killing healthy cells. It attaches to the genetic makeup of the cells themselves and masquerades as healthy cell structure. HIV is also a highly adaptive virus, changing forms not only within populations but also mutating within individuals. Finding financing for vaccine research is also difficult, since many drug companies are invested in developing treatment options. The development of a vaccine can therefore take enormous resources but is extremely risky in terms of payoff.

Scientists also note that immunizations typically rely on injecting individuals with a "watered down" version of a disease so that a person basically gets a mild form of it and then develops

> " Any effective initiative to combat the spread of AIDS must mobilize effective enforcement of criminal laws by local officials in order to eliminate the market for sex trafficking and drastically reduce the instances of rape and other sexual assaults."
>
> **Gary Haugen**
> **President**
> **International**
> **Justice Mission**

immunities. But those vaccines are usually developed by studying individuals who have survived the infection and whose bodies have developed natural immunities. While individuals with HIV can greatly reduce the rate of infection through the use of antiretroviral drugs, no one has been found to be virus-free once they have contracted the disease.

In 1996, the International AIDS Vaccine Initiative (IAVI) was founded in order to increase attention on the search for a vaccine as well as to coordinate efforts in research.

The IAVI is an international nonprofit organization which tracks the work of teams doing research in several countries, allowing scientists to try different approaches to finding a vaccine so that no one course is taken exclusively. It also encourages the sharing of information among researchers and helps teams of scientists progress through clinical trials. IAVI also insists that any vaccine developed with its support be made available in developing countries at reasonable prices, rapidly, and in sufficient quantity. This removes some of the profit incentive that normally spurs drug research, but also guarantees that any vaccine that is developed would go to where the need is greatest.

But some who have studied the disease warn that its adaptive nature could make it drug-resistant to any vaccine within a relatively short time frame. This would mean an individual who had been immunized could still be infected by a resistant strain or a mutation of the disease. This might lead to even greater problems, such as people taking fewer precautions, or strains developing that would not respond to treatments. And because of

FACT:

In Russia, heroin is often cheaper than alcohol and is one of the primary reasons HIV infections have risen dramatically.

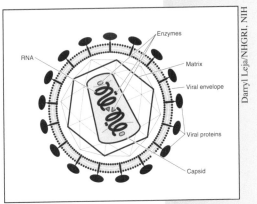

Darryl Leja/NHGRI, NIH

Structure of Human Immunodeficiency Virus (HIV)

Three Squabbles
that Dominate AIDS Reporting

If you've read the newspaper lately, you've probably seen one or more of these issues discussed. Very briefly, here's what they are all about.

The Global Fund vs. the US Government

1. The Global Fund was established as a way to bring funds together and funnel them to country programs in order to fight AIDS efficiently. In 2003, the US decided to let the newly created Global AIDS Coordinator decide how to spend most of the funds budgeted for AIDS in order to have more control over programs and countries funded. Some internationalists say the US is being too nationalistic; the US says the Global Fund isn't efficient enough to handle such a large infusion of money. The US Government has also said that it does not want to contribute more to the Global Fund until all countries are contributing a portion commensurate with their ability to pay. (See discussion on pages 47-52).

Abstinence vs. Condoms

2. Abstinence and condom use are two ways to prevent the spread of HIV infections. Abstinence is often the method preferred by faith-based organizations and has been encouraged by US government-funded programs after studies showed its effectiveness in Uganda and other countries. The use of condoms is promoted by many organizations who feel abstinence doesn't work and is based on studies that lack scientific rigor. Pro-abstinence people say delaying sex confers many health benefits, especially for young people, and that condoms, even when available, are rarely used properly or regularly. Pro-condom people say that they haven't been distributed widely enough or used long enough to be accurately evaluated. (See discussion on pages 24-26).

Generic vs. Brand Name Drugs

3. Most AIDS drugs were developed by western pharmaceutical companies, and under international law have patent protection for twenty years. But they tend to be more costly than the generic drugs produced in countries such as India that may violate patent protection. The US will not allow the use of government funds to purchase drugs unless they are approved by the FDA, which has led to accusations that the US is protecting business interests over saving lives. The US position is that it does not want to encourage the distribution of drugs that may be unsafe. This is complicated by the fact that one generic drug combines three different drug treatments into one pill and has become very popular in developing countries, but is manufactured by an Indian drug company which has so far not submitted for FDA approval. The Doha agreement is also related to this discussion, which is further discussed on page 53.

the different strains of the virus, it is possible that a vaccine might be developed that would be effective on one strain but not others.

Finally, public health officials point out that even if an effective vaccine was discovered soon, it would take a massive effort to produce the vaccine and immunize populations. But we would still need to deal with the forty-two million people already infected.

Are there different types of drugs to treat HIV/AIDS?

■ Drugs to treat HIV/AIDS are called antiretroviral (ARV) drugs and act by stopping the HIV from reproducing inside the body, thereby giving the immune system a chance to fight back. There are three main types of ARVs.

Nucleoside Reverse Transcriptase Inhibitors (known as "Nukes") mimic the process the virus uses to invade the cells and then stop replications of the HIV. Two of the more common drugs, AZT and 3TC, are Nukes.

The second group are Non-Nucleoside Reverse Transcriptase Inhibitors, known as "Non-Nukes" because they work by blocking a part of the enzyme necessary to produce the viral DNA.

The third group is known as Protease Inhibitors because they prevent the viral particles from maturing.

A cocktail of three or more drugs is known as Highly Active Antiretroviral Therapy (HAART) and is often used with people who have developed AIDS. Studies show that use of this drug therapy can reduce illness and death by as much as 70 percent.

Reuters

Chemist in Bombay works on new vaccine.

What is meant by retrovirus and lentivirus?

■ HIV is both a retrovirus and a lentivirus. A retrovirus stores its genetic information on a single-stranded RNA molecule instead of the double-stranded DNA, which is more common. After a retrovirus penetrates a cell, it uses a special enzyme called a reverse transcriptase to construct a DNA version of its genes which then is incorporated into the cell's own genetic material. A lentivirus produces a chronic disease in its host and can remain latent for long periods of time. The time between infection and symptoms can lag by months or years. A lentivirus is a type of retrovirus.

If a person thinks he or she has been infected to HIV/AIDS is there anything that can be done?

■ A treatment known as Post-Exposure Prophylaxis (PEP) can be administered to a person who may not have tested positive for HIV but has been exposed within the last seventy-two hours through rape or injury, such as a health-worker being pricked by a needle containing infected blood. Some studies seem to indicate that treatment with ARVs reduces the chances that a person may become infected. But there is also concern that such treatments could foster drug resistance, since they are typically only administered for a short period of time.

Does a person always contract HIV if they have sex with an infected person?

■ No, the infection rate varies depending on the method of transmission, although a person can be infected by only one contact. Male to male sexual relations tend to transmit the virus more efficiently than male to female. An infected woman is less likely to infect a man than an infected man is to infect a woman. But because IV drug use is a relatively efficient means of infection, those who become infected this way often pass on the infection to their sexual partner before they realize they have contracted the disease. So when drug use is the primary method of infection, HIV may spread rapidly through the population associated with the drug user.

What are the side effects of drug treatments for HIV/AIDS?

■ Side effects vary by drug and individual, but may include nausea and headaches or more serious side effects. It is important to monitor the side effects in order to adjust dosage or to help determine if a different drug will be more effective. Additionally, the most serious problem is when a person begins to develop immunity to the particular drug therapy.

Isn't it true that Africans and people in other developing countries don't have the ability to take the drugs properly?

■ Antiretroviral drugs do need some supervision to be administered properly, but do not need as high a level of care as was once thought. Early treatment courses of ARVs were complex, especially those taken in combinations. Now some drugs are combined into a single pill that can be taken as little as once a day. It is important for a person seeking treatment to be tested accurately and for the treatment to be monitored enough to know whether the drug therapy is working. Side effects must also be monitored.

In a recent trial in Uganda, 97 percent of the participants were consistent in their treatment, demonstrating a high level of compliance.

Another challenge is that there are so few health workers available in many countries. Almost every developing country is experiencing a severe shortage of health workers.

Why can't drugs be made available to all pregnant women who are at risk?

■ Some doctors suggest that every pregnant woman in highly infected countries receive at least a single dosage of an antiretroviral drug to help reduce the transmission rate to infants. But even that has become controversial, since ethicists question why a woman would be provided with enough drugs to prevent transmission to the baby, but not enough to prolong her life so she could care for the child.

Many drugs have side effects. There may be some risks associated with taking ARVs; therefore, a woman who has not been tested might be concerned about the risk of taking a drug if she was not sure she needed it to prevent transmission.

What is the 3 x 5 Initiative?

■ The 3 x 5 Initiative is the name given to a goal set by the World Health Organization to reach three million infected people with ARV treatments by 2005. The strategy for accomplishing this goal includes five pillars: Global leadership; strong partnership and advocacy; urgent, sustained country support; simplified, standardized tools for delivering ARV therapy; effective, reliable supply of medicines and diagnostics; and rapid identification and reapplication of new knowledge and successes.

What is the "Lazarus Effect"?

■ This is a term developed during the time when ARVs were first made available to those dealing with AIDS. A person who had lost considerable weight and was dealing with secondary infections was able to make a rapid and remarkable recovery by receiving ARVs. In essence, the person appeared to rise from his or her death bed. This dramatic response to treatment, especially for those with very visible signs of AIDS, helped make ARVs popular.

Is the US blood supply really safe?

■ The Red Cross goes to great lengths to ensure that the blood supply is free of hepatitis, HIV, and other diseases. The pre-screening process for potential donors is far more extensive than in the past and disqualifies people who have visited countries with high rates of HIV infection and even people who lived in Europe for more than six months during certain periods of time.

In addition, every donation is tested using highly sensitive techniques that are able to detect viruses at a very early point in development. The blood supply in the US is considered to be completely safe, although all the additional screening has created an ongoing shortage of blood. Because of this, some doctors recommend "banking" blood before an operation in order to ensure availability more than safety.

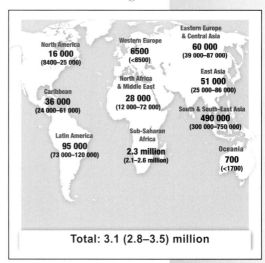

UNAIDS/WHO

North America
16 000
(8400–25 000)

Western Europe
6500
(<8500)

Eastern Europe & Central Asia
60 000
(39 000–87 000)

North Africa & Middle East
28 000
(12 000–72 000)

East Asia
51 000
(25 000–86 000)

Caribbean
36 000
(24 000–61 000)

South & South-East Asia
490 000
(300 000–750 000)

Latin America
95 000
(73 000–120 000)

Sub-Saharan Africa
2.3 million
(2.1–2.6 million)

Oceania
700
(<1700)

Total: 3.1 (2.8–3.5) million

Estimated adult and child deaths due to HIV/AIDS during 2004

A small loan made it possible for this woman to start her own business in Cambodia.

ECONOMIC IMPACT

Many discussions about AIDS include talk about money. Here are some of the questions people have about the economics of AIDS.

Does the HIV/AIDS situation in other parts of the world have any effect on the US economy?

■ Most economists believe that in today's world, we live in a global economy in which every nation's economic health impacts the others. The global AIDS crisis has devastated many economies in poor and developing countries. This means that those countries are more vulnerable to famines, wars, political instability, and declining standards of living.

As the crisis spreads, it is beginning to affect such countries as India, China, and Russia, all of which represent markets, trading partners, and sources of labor for the US.

The CIA has identified the AIDS crisis as a threat to national security because of its destabilizing effects on economies and governments and because it helps widen the gap between relatively wealthy and poor nations. And since AIDS is growing rapidly in nations with economic clout and even nuclear weapons, there is a perception that it is in the long term political and economic interests of the US to be on the forefront of preventing and treating those with AIDS.

Finally, it is far more economically beneficial to prevent HIV infections than to treat people with AIDS or to deal with the consequences of widespread illness and mortality.

FACT:

AIDS will have claimed the lives of at least one-fifth of agricultural workers in southern Africa by 2020.

What are the "next wave" countries?

■ China, India, Russia, Ethiopia, and Nigeria were identified as the "next wave" countries in the HIV/AIDS pandemic by the National Intelligence Council in 2002. The designation was given to them because all have significant and growing infection rates, large populations, and governments that had not given fighting the disease a high priority. These countries account for nearly 40 percent of the world's population, and the report showed that their infections could grow to as high as 75 million people in 2010. India already has the largest number of infected people of any country outside Africa.

Why does AIDS hit the economies so hard?

■ Most people affected by HIV/AIDS are in the prime of life. They are the most productive workers, parents of young children, and are earning the most wages. They are the backbone of the economies of most countries.

In most developing countries, agriculture is the primary livelihood. According to UNAIDS, agriculture accounts for 70 percent of Africa's employment. Agriculture is very labor intensive and not only provides wages for the workers but also produces food for their families. If a worker is ill, there is often no one to take his place, so the ground lies fallow. If a crop isn't planted on time a family or an entire village may miss the harvest. The food from that harvest may have been counted on to supply food for the rest of the year. Likewise, food from each family's plot of land may have been pooled to support the entire village, so as there is a decrease in contribution to the pooled grain bank, the amount of food available to the village may decline.

"
AIDS was not understood in the same way by everyone in the church, but they are changing. . . . Our church members now know how to welcome a person with AIDS in to the church as a human being."

Juvenal Ngedahayo
Association des
Eglise Inkuru Nziza
Kigali, Rwanda

The World Bank is also tracking the impact of HIV/AIDS in other sectors of the economy and has found significant costs associated with absenteeism, lower productivity, employee turnover, increased training, and recruitment costs. And the public sector is affected in many countries by a severe shortage of teachers and health workers attributed to the AIDS crisis.

As more and more adults fall ill and die, their children are taken in by family members and others. Many families in Africa now include a large number of children. So in a typical village, there are fewer adults to work and more children to care for. Often the caretakers are older people who are no longer able to be very productive. Sometimes young people will leave the village to seek jobs in the city. But too often those young people end up in low-paying jobs or are forced into prostitution.

This cycle has contributed to famine in some countries and to widespread malnutrition.

Are the costs of these problems actually measured?

■ Like most statistics associated with AIDS, the figures are approximates, but there are measurements done by such groups as the World Bank, the Food and Agriculture Organization (FAO), and the International Labor Organization (ILO). For example, the ILO projects that the labor force in thirty-eight countries (most in Africa) will decline by between 5 and 35 percent by 2020 due to the effects of AIDS. Statistics are mostly available by region or country and measure decline in worker productivity, labor force, and gross domestic product.

Other ways to measure the impact include the rising number of children in the labor force, the decline in savings levels, and the sale of family assets in order to care for sick family members or pay funeral expenses.

FACT:

Amnesty International estimates that 135 million women and girls worldwide have undergone genital mutilation.

What are some of the other effects on families and individuals in developing countries?

▪ Having someone in the family who is ill often takes a situation that is already difficult and makes it catastrophic. If the person is the primary wage earner, the family can lose all their income and their primary source of food. Children often must stop going to school because they can no longer pay the school fees. Other results include a high risk of sexual and labor exploitation of women and children who are desperate for food and basic necessities. When a member of the family dies, funeral costs can put the family into debt. Illness and death associated with HIV/AIDS causes a downward spiral for a family, not only reducing their current income and standard of living but also robbing their future chances of moving out of poverty.

What is "transactional sex"?

▪ Transactional sex refers to anytime sex is exchanged for something of value, including money, food, or shelter. It refers to everything from formal prostitution to the relationship some young women have with older men in poor countries in which their education is paid for as long as they are willing to have sex with the man.

What is "survival sex"?

▪ The term is somewhat controversial but is used by some to mean either commercial or occasional sexual activity engaged in out of economic desperation. Because of the desperate poverty in many countries and the fact that women often have few or no rights, some are either forced or coerced into sexual relations in order to feed themselves or their children. Also, children who are orphaned and end up living on the streets sometimes survive by offering sex to adults in exchange for money, food, or shelter.

Some organizations and individuals use this term to distinguish individuals who engage in such activities as a last resort from those who make the choice to be sex workers.

How does labor migration contribute to the pandemic?

■ In Africa and other poor areas of the world, it is common for people to move toward large cities and areas where labor is needed. Sometimes people become migrant farm workers. In Africa, large numbers of laborers were needed in mining and were brought from rural areas to provide inexpensive and plentiful labor.

Because migrant workers are typically men and are away from their families for long periods of time, it is common for prostitutes to congregate in areas where migrant workers live. When the men go home, they may bring with them STDs, including HIV. Based on patterns of infection, it seems clear that the rate of HIV infection follows paths of migrant workers.

Another pattern of disease runs along the transportation routes in Africa. This seems to indicate that infected truckers spread HIV across a region and among countries. As truckers move across regions, they are often stopped at border crossings and checkpoints for days at a time as they go through immigration and customs formalities. These checkpoints attract prostitutes and petty traders.

Power of Love

This father is fortunate to live and work near his family.

Labor migration also occurs in Asia, where young people are sometimes lured from rural areas with promises of jobs only to find that they are expected to become prostitutes. In China, India, and former Soviet countries, individuals often move seeking better jobs, but only find greater poverty. Labor migration is found wherever poverty exists. It almost always breaks down the social and cultural structure and has been responsible for the spread of diseases for decades.

What is micro-enterprise and how does it help poor women?

■ Micro-enterprise, also called microfinance, is a method whereby poor people are given small loans to help them finance a business. The loans may be as little as $50 and are given to individuals to help them start such businesses as selling vegetables in a market, developing a sewing business, buying tools in order to provide services, or purchasing soda for resale. The loans are usually made to people who cannot qualify for commercial loans or who would be charged an exorbitant rate if they did apply for a loan. Many individuals who begin with small loans are able to develop their businesses into enterprises that can provide income for their entire family.

Micro-enterprise is especially helpful for women who have typically relied on their husbands to provide food or income. Some micro-enterprise organizations are providing training to young people whose parents are sick or have died so that they can earn a living independently.

Most micro-enterprise organizations are supported by nonprofit groups which help provide the initial capital for the loans. Eventually, the loan funds can become self-sustaining and may even become commercial banks which can provide loans and also accept savings while still dealing primarily with the very poor.

How does micro-enterprise relate to the AIDS crisis?

■ Micro-enterprise is typically carried out in small groups which work together to guarantee each other's loans and provide support during regular meetings. These meetings also provide opportunity for education, especially in the basics of business and health. Because nonprofit organizations typically provide the structure for these groups, they are able to use them as a way to teach AIDS education, especially to women. And because there is a certain amount of group support and pressure, women can learn to stand up for their rights, including asking their husbands to be faithful or use condoms if they suspect them to be HIV infected.

Also, women who have some measure of economic independence are not as likely to succumb to pressure from men to have sex in exchange for food, education, or shelter. They are more readily able to find work near their home instead of migrating to cities where they may end up in prostitution.

Microfinance has been so successful in some countries that it has had an impact on the overall economy of the nation. It has helped spur growth outside of cities and has been especially helpful in providing a means whereby women caring for many children can earn an income while staying close to home.

What does debt forgiveness have to do with AIDS?

■ Many poor countries have an enormous debt burden created by borrowing over the last decades. Some of these funds were borrowed by corrupt leaders who used the money to finance their own lifestyles. Other funds were borrowed to fund civic projects, but the interest rates were so high that the burden of the debt became too great.

About 40,000 new HIV infections occur each year in the US.

Some believe that money was loaned to these countries at very high rates of interest and without concern about what the debt would do to the countries. It would be a little like a bank offering a loan for a million dollar home to a family earning very little money each year. The chances of default would be great. In the US, the family would be protected from entering into such an agreement because it would take their entire income just to cover the interest payment each year, but of course poor countries have no such protection.

In order to repay their debts, many countries must rob themselves of badly needed funds to provide for transportation, public health, education, and communication. Without this infrastructure, it is difficult to combat AIDS. Jubilee 2000 was a campaign embraced by many humanitarian organizations, religious groups, and some governments. Its aim was to promote debt forgiveness in exchange for guarantees that the money would instead go to alleviate poverty. The singer Bono was very involved in this campaign and has also been an outspoken advocate of helping fund AIDS work in developing countries.

What about charities? Aren't many of them concentrating on fighting AIDS?

■ Many international charities have made AIDS one of their primary causes. No matter what the emphasis of the organization, AIDS has an effect on the people they serve. In the US, many groups have received substantial grants through USAID and other government agencies to provide assistance. They have also received funding from foundations and large donors. But most would say that individual donors have not supported the cause as much as other needs. Some religious groups find that their donors are still reluctant to help fund a cause which they view as being caused by immoral behavior. Others admit that their American donors are simply apathetic to a cause that gets little media attention and seems to be surrounded by controversy.

What is the Global Fund?

■ The Global Fund for Tuberculosis, AIDS, and Malaria (GFTAM, or the Global Fund) was launched in 2001 with the help of the UN and promoted by Kofi Annan, UN Secretary General. It was envisioned as an international partnership of public and private interests to help funnel funds directly to countries fighting the three diseases. Because it would offer a coordinated mechanism, the hope was that this one fund would provide an

Of the AIDS-related deaths in the US in 2002, more than half were among blacks.

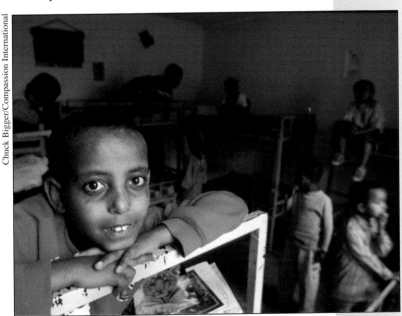

Chuck Bigger/Compassion International

efficient method for funding prevention and treatment at the local level. Funds have come not only from governments but also from the Gates Foundation, the Rockefeller Foundation, and the Clinton Foundation. The fund has a board of direc-

Nine-year-old Said lives with 20 other HIV positive children in a Christian home in Addis Ababa, Ethiopia.

tors made up of representatives from governments, the private sector, NGOs, and has a small staff originally seconded from UNAIDS and WHO.

Of the $15 billion promised by the Bush administration under the President's Emergency Plan for AIDS Relief (PEPFAR), less than $300 million per year would go to the Global Fund. This has been viewed as an indication that the US is not truly supportive of the fund. The Fund has fallen short of its goal to raise $10 billion per year in order to fight AIDS.

It sounds like a great deal of money is being spent on AIDS. Is more really needed?

■ It's true that a great deal of money is going to fight the war on AIDS. According to UNAIDS, nearly $5 billion was spent on fighting AIDS in the developing world during 2003. But estimates are that $12 billion will be needed annually by 2005 for prevention, treatment and support of those in poor countries. And the amount rises to $20 billion per year by 2007.

The $20 billion would provide counseling and testing for one hundred million adults, treat six million infected people with antiretroviral drugs, care for twenty-two million orphans, and provide school-based AIDS education for nine hundred million students, as well as peer counseling for another sixty million young people not in school.

Is all that money going to Africa?

■ No. Less than half would go to Africa by 2007 since the HIV infection rate is increasing rapidly in other parts of the world. Asia will need 28 percent of the funds, 17 percent would go to Latin America and the Caribbean, 9 percent to Eastern Europe, and the rest would go to Africa, mostly in sub-Saharan countries.

How can we be sure the money is being used efficiently?

■ Most programs administered by the UN or through US grants have very specific requirements for reporting and meeting goals. Interim reports evaluate progress in meeting the goals and additional funding is not released until specific goals are met. The Global Fund's progress in allocating and monitoring funds is closely scrutinized by the governments, corporations, and NGOs that make up the board of directors and provide the funds. Almost all government and large foundation grants have very stringent requirements for not only when reports must be filed, but also what documentation must be included and the verification of progress by objective parties.

FACT:

In Uganda, the national prevalence rate dropped from 12 percent in the early 1990s to 4.1 percent in 2003.

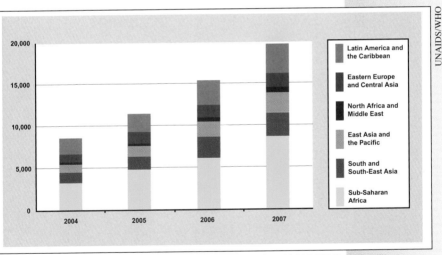

UNAIDS/WHO

Legend:
- Latin America and the Caribbean
- Eastern Europe and Central Asia
- North Africa and Middle East
- East Asia and the Pacific
- South and South-East Asia
- Sub-Saharan Africa

Projected annual HIV and AIDS financing needs by region, 2004-2007 (in US$ million)

Isn't the US giving more than anyone else?

■ According to a report by UNAIDS and the Organization for Economic Development and Cooperation (OECD), the US is the single largest national donor, followed by the UK, Japan, and the Netherlands.

What types of programs are supported by the funds?

■ Funds support HIV/AIDS prevention, testing, treatment, and care services, as well as social and legal assistance to those affected by the pandemic.

So why is there so much controversy about the money the US is giving?

■ In 2003, the US government pledged to give $15 billion to fight AIDS over the next five years. By all measures, this was a very generous and important gift, but several issues soon arose.

First, instead of giving it through the Global Fund, the US decided to give only $1 billion of the money over five years to the Fund. The rest is to be distributed primarily through a new office of the Global AIDS Coordinator, established in the Department of State and with much of the money flowing through the United States Agency for International Development (USAID). This frustrated international AIDS officials who felt that the best way to fight the pandemic was to pool resources so that groups did not compete or duplicate work and priorities could be set globally. But the US felt that the Global Fund was not necessarily distributing money as efficiently as it had planned and wanted to use its own methods for getting funding to those affected.

Second, there has been some concern that funds budgeted for the new AIDS initiative would have to come from cuts in other humanitarian funds. The aid community felt that it was counter-productive to borrow from programs such as maternal health, education, or child survival to fund the HIV/AIDS budget.

Third, the US government decided to focus the new AIDS initiative on fifteen countries—most of them in Africa. Critics felt that the criteria for country selection was not apparent and seemed based more on politics than need, since many countries with high HIV/AIDS infection rates were not included. The US government maintained that focusing on these countries would offer better results.

Another controversy has arisen over the new US government policy to focus HIV/AIDS prevention funding on programs that include promotion of abstinence and monogamy. Previously, the major component of US-funded prevention programs was condom distribution. The US policy change was

Only 1.5 percent of vulnerable adults in Eastern Europe are voluntarily tested for HIV.

Children enjoy a puppet show in Cambodia which teaches them about AIDS at an early age.

based on evidence from African countries, primarily Uganda, that showed abstinence by youth and increased faithfulness among sexually active men were both more significant factors in causing HIV/AIDS to decline, than was condom use. Many critics of this policy change viewed the emphasis on abstinence as unrealistic in poor countries and part of a politically and religiously conservative agenda. Others believed that more attention should have been given to other prevention methods and treatment for those already infected.

Finally, there has been great international frustration over the inability to obtain drug treatments at a reasonable price. Name brand antiretroviral drugs are several times more expensive than generic drugs, even though many of the generics have the same chemical properties and are approved by the WHO and UNAIDS. The US government has insisted that its fund be used only for name brand drugs, based on concerns for safety and efficacy. This means that far fewer people would be able to be treated through US government-funded programs than if generics were allowed. Furthermore, the WHO and UNAIDS have approved generic "fixed-dose combinations" for treatment. This combines the ingredients of the three-drug "cocktails" into one dose which can be more easily managed by the patient and would be especially helpful in developing countries. Such combinations aren't yet marketed by any of the major pharmaceutical companies.

The US government has now approved the use of generic drugs in programs funded by government grants as long as the drugs pass through a Food and Drug Administration (FDA) approval process. But critics complain that this process is basically identical to the WHO pre-qualification process and is simply another delaying tactic.

What is the World Trade Organization and what does it have to do with all this?

■ The World Trade Organization (WTO) sets the rules, enables trade, and negotiates disputes between member countries. It is the primary body overseeing international trade agreements.

The WTO's main involvement has been in relation to the intellectual property rights of pharmaceutical companies and whether countries can violate the patents in order to have access to life-saving generic drugs. Under the Trade Related Aspects of Intellectual Property Rights Agreement (TRIPS) all countries must comply with patent protection measures involving drugs. However, under what has become known as the Doha Declaration (because it occurred during a WTO meeting in Doha, Qatar), a provision of the agreement which allows countries to declare a public health emergency and thereby bypass certain patent protections was clarified and affirmed. It is the Doha Declaration that permits countries to legally manufacture or import generic drugs under "compulsory licenses" before patent protections have expired.

FACT:

India has the largest number of people living with HIV outside South Africa— 5.1 million.

UN AIDS/WHO

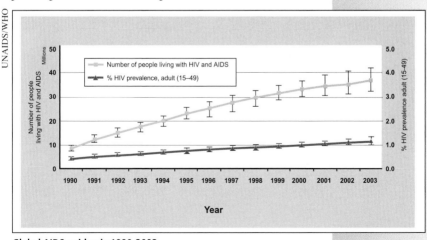

Global AIDS epidemic 1990-2003

A grandmother cares for her grandchild in Zambia, a common sight throughout Africa.

CULTURE AND PRACTICE

When discussing issues of culture and belief, it's important to acknowledge that we approach such questions with our own set of beliefs, norms, prejudices, and expectations. Perhaps one of the biggest challenges we all face is recognizing that many of the people affected by HIV/AIDS have neither our experience of the past nor our expectations for the future.

Why are there so many AIDS orphans?

■ An orphan is a child under the age of fifteen who has lost one or both parents. According to the 2004 report of UNAIDS, there are twelve million children in sub-Saharan Africa and fourteen million worldwide who are orphans due to AIDS.

The number is so high because HIV-infected people are typically of childbearing age. Women are often infected by their husbands and may find out they are infected only after giving birth to a child who is obviously sick.

It seems like there have been different numbers reported on orphans. Why is there confusion?

■ Part of the confusion arises because children are not often identified publicly as AIDS orphans since that stigmatizes them and the families who care for them. The current and projected number of orphans, just like all AIDS data, is estimated through statistical models. The modeling techniques have improved over the years, and many experts have now begun to agree on the various assumptions to include in the models. As the

FACT:

Although prostitution is illegal in Thailand, the Thai government provided AIDS education to sex workers and encouraged use of condoms, all part of reducing the HIV infection level significantly in that country.

methodologies develop and the information on which assumptions are based improves, the numbers change but are increasingly more reliable.

Orphans are also described in different ways. There are more than one hundred million orphans in the world, using the UN definition, but that number includes children who have been orphaned due to wars, disease, and other factors. To distinguish just those children orphaned by AIDS can be difficult.

Finally, children may lose one parent and continue to live with the other or may be abandoned or sent to live with relatives because the other parent is too ill to care for them. Or, if the mother dies, the father may be working far away and not be able to care for the children. Typically, when one parent dies, the other is infected and is ill or dying as well. For these reasons, a child who loses one parent to AIDS—whether a father or mother—is considered an orphan.

Is the number of orphans expected to increase?

■ Yes. Even if the infection rate begins to slow down, unless there is widespread use of ARVs, the number of orphans will continue to increase for years after the infection rate slows. In Uganda, where the HIV prevalence rate peaked nearly ten years ago, the number of orphans is just now reaching its peak.

What is happening to all these children?

■ The vast majority of AIDS orphans live in Africa, where children are traditionally cared for by relatives. This means that families are being strained to deal with the many additional dependents. Sometimes grandparents are caring for their grandchildren after their sons and daughters have died.

Increasingly, there are households where the oldest sister or brother cares for the younger children.

Are orphanages the best solution?

■ Over the years, African culture has never accepted the concept of orphanages because it is such a strong tradition for families to care for the children of relatives or friends. But as families are being overwhelmed by the cost of caring for so many children and as more child-headed households spring up, there are more discussions about how to care for children in a way that respects tradition but also provides basic care.

There have been some experiments with foster living arrangements where groups of children are cared for by resident adults who allow them to remain with their closest relatives but also provide for their support. This is especially effective in villages where children can remain near their homes and be in a familiar situation.

Most experts on childcare worldwide agree that institutional care is much less desirable for the healthy development of children than some kind of family care. Institutional childcare has been abandoned in most developed countries because of concerns both about the quality of care and costs. Furthermore, orphanages would simply not be a financially viable option for developing countries at the scale required. It costs much more to care for a child in an institution than in a family, and neither governments nor charities

FACT:

In Botswana life expectancy decreased from 65 years in 1985–1990 to 40 years in 2000–2005.

Reuters

HIV positive orphans in Kenya wait for services from private aid group.

Can AIDS orphans be adopted?

■ Many countries have laws against foreign adoptions, especially in African countries by non-Africans. This is partially due to the fact that family ties are so important to Africans that they would feel a child was better off with a friend or distant relative even if the child did not receive an education or what we might consider a decent standard of living.

Children carry on traditions, inherit the land, and are keepers of the family name and honor. To leave the family is to lose the things a child considers most dear. Sometimes it is hard for Americans to understand that our views of what is important are not the same as those of people in developing countries.

Is it true that there is a crisis in dealing with the elderly in some countries?

■ Yes, in many cultures it is expected that children will care for their elders. But when so many men and women in their twenties and thirties are dying, their parents have no one to care for them as they age. Since life expectancy is much lower in many developing countries, a person may be elderly in his or her fifties, especially since there may have been little health care and poor nutrition.

There are no retirement homes in most countries, nor is there Social Security or pension plans. People who are too old to work or find their own food are totally dependent on younger people. But in many countries, those who are older are caring for their grandchildren and are barely able to cope. Older people who were once revered are now left to fend for themselves.

> **"Globalization, travel, and migration add to the risk of increased spread to what we might think of as 'safe' countries. The reality is that in our globalized world, there are no 'safe' countries."**
>
> **Louise Frechette**
> UN deputy secretary general

What other cultural issues are affected by or affect the spread of HIV/AIDS?

■ There are certain African customs that have spread AIDS, especially through families. One is that if a woman's husband dies, she is expected to have sex with one of his relatives. Sometimes she is expected to become another wife for him; in other cases she is said to be purified of her husband's death by having sex with a relative. This tradition comes from the belief that a family should be cared for by other family members, and if a man dies, his wife and children are "inherited" along with his property.

There is also a custom that young women and girls are to provide sex for an older male relative if he has no wife. This is also seen as a way to thank the relative for providing for the immediate family's needs.

Also, there is the widespread belief that a woman's worth is primarily related to her ability to bear children. This is one of the reasons a woman does not like to ask a man to use a condom.

In Latin and Asian cultures, women are often considered subservient to men and have few rights. They find their value in being married and having children.

Why aren't condoms more effective in preventing HIV/AIDS?

■ Condom distribution systems aren't very efficient in developing countries, creating gaps in supply and also exposing condoms to long periods of storage and transportation in temperatures and other conditions that can damage them. Even at subsidized prices, condoms can be too expensive for regular use by the majority of people.

FACT:

Even though Uganda has significantly reduced the rate of HIV infections, its AIDS orphan population continues to grow because previously infected people continue to die.

Most men feel condoms take away from the pleasure of sex, and men in developing countries find condoms to be completely foreign to their experience. American men, on the other hand, grew up with condoms and as teenagers may have carried a condom as a sign that they were sexually active.

In a culture where making a woman pregnant is enormously valued, such as in Africa, men have never used condoms, and women have rarely used birth control of any kind.

Men in developing countries also lack access to drug stores or other places where condoms are easily purchased. They often don't have places to store condoms where they will not be exposed to heat, sun, and other elements. Condoms distributed in Africa are typically white latex, which feels foreign to African men. But condoms are not popular in Asia or Eastern Europe, either, even among those who are HIV infected.

Many public health officials and women's advocates believe that more should be done to develop an effective method for women to use in order to protect themselves from infection.

What are some of the other cultural factors affecting women?

■ As previously discussed, in almost all developing countries of the world, women have few rights and choices in life. Many countries give them little legal protection and most societies view them as being responsible for making their husbands happy, bearing children, and caring for the family.

Where countries do have laws protecting women's rights, these rights have often not permeated male-dominated cultural beliefs and traditions. Often domestic violence against women is not reported or prosecuted. Surveys done in some

African countries reveal that both men and women believe that a husband has the right to beat his wife. Women have reported being beaten for asking their husbands about extramarital sexual activity or for requesting them to use condoms.

Women marry at very early ages and begin to have children as quickly as possible. A woman typically values having many children, both because of the high rate of child mortality and the fact that it is important for families to have many children in order to help provide for the family and strengthen the family legacy. Women often have difficulties in childbearing since there are few doctors or medical facilities to offer help.

In situations where women are alone or girls are orphaned, it is easy for predators to force them into prostitution, enslave them as laborers, or even force them to become child soldiers.

What are child soldiers?

■ Increasingly, rebel groups and others are either kidnapping children or attracting vulnerable children to join their cause and become soldiers or provide sex for soldiers. Child soldiers are defined by UNICEF as anyone under the age of eighteen who is part of a regular or irregular fighting force. It is estimated that there are 300,000 child soldiers worldwide. Girls who become child soldiers are often subjected to sexual violence and are vulnerable to becoming infected with STDs, including HIV.

What is meant by "vulnerable populations"?

■ In the context of HIV/AIDS, vulnerable populations are defined by UNAIDS as groups that: are denied their human rights; have limited access to HIV information, health service, and means of prevention; and/or have limited ability to negotiate

FACT:

HIV prevalence among injecting drug users can rise to 40 percent or more within one to two years of the introduction of the virus into their communities.

safer sex. In most countries this means women and girls, the poor, certain ethnic groups, and refugees.

Why do people believe the rumors that having sex with a virgin cures AIDS?

■ When we first hear about such an obviously false rumor, it is easy to assume that people who believe such things are different from us. But when you realize that most people in developing countries have little formal education, no access to regular formal information such as the newspaper, and no system of law that requires people to avoid making false claims, it begins to be more understandable.

In the absence of formal health care, many poor people turn to traditional healers, who may be a cross between a doctor and a minister. Some are very good and promote practices that save lives and improve healing. Sociologists and anthropologists can point to many times when "educated minds" have dismissed claims of natural remedies only to eventually come back around to their effectiveness.

But traditional healers do not attend medical school and are not licensed. Some are very good and ethical, but others seek to control people and extract a livelihood from illnesses. Traditional healers have recommended many "cures" for HIV/AIDS because it is not in their interests to say the disease is incurable. Public health officials are now beginning to train some traditional healers so that they can incorporate sound medical advice into their traditional healing practices.

Finally, just as people with fatal diseases in any country will try almost any type of medication or promise of a cure, so people in developing countries will naturally become more and more desperate as they see the people around them die of the same disease. One of the reasons it is so important

> " Increased access to treatment is one of the most powerful incentives for individuals to learn their HIV status."
> **UNAIDS/WHO AIDS Epidemic Update December 2003**

to provide medical treatment in developing countries is so infected people seek dependable and proven treatment.

Is it true that many people still believe in witchcraft?

■ Yes, people of all religions sometimes also rely on forms of witchcraft, just as people in this country might read their horoscope. In some cases, witchcraft is used to describe what we might call evil. It is a force for all bad things. Without clear explanations of cause and effect, it is easier to assume a particular force is in control. Witch doctors are often happy to help spread rumors of such a force so that they can sell potions or remedies for combating witchcraft. But some so-called witch doctors are really closer to traditional healers, providing recipes to cure ailments.

Why would some people think AIDS is a plot launched by Americans?

■ Many Africans are grateful for the help provided by Americans. However, in many countries there is a history of fear and mistrust from the days of colonialism. At times, America has been viewed as exploiting certain countries for their natural resources or helping to bring about changes in leadership by encouraging coups. In 2001, Muammar Qadhafi, president of Libya, charged that AIDS was created in a CIA laboratory. Other leaders have made similar claims.

While it sounds preposterous, the fact that some published reports suggested that HIV may have actually jumped from monkeys to humans through a vaccine program in Africa helps fuel such concerns. And in South Africa there is evidence that a white scientist developed biological warfare

FACT:

HIV and tuberculosis are sometimes called the "terrible twins."

during the apartheid regime in the 1980s and may have encouraged HIV-infected individuals to infect the black population.

Some in Africa joke that AIDS stands for American Invention to Discourage Sex, and still stereotype Americans as the puritanical missionaries of the 1940s who asked Africans to conform to American norms.

Do people of certain religions have a lower incidence of AIDS?

■ Religion plays a role in the pandemic on many levels. Some religions encourage certain behaviors that seem to correlate to a lower rate of infection. Some religious leaders have been more involved in AIDS education than others. And some religions interpret their beliefs in ways that are more or less helpful to the spread of AIDS.

There have been some studies in Africa showing that observant Muslims have a lower infection rate than other religions, even when measured in the same region. This is largely attributed to the fact that Muslim men tend to be circumcised—a practice that seems to slow infection and transmission of the disease—while Christian and men following traditional religions tend not to be. (More scientific studies are being done to verify this connection.) But it may also be attributed to the fact that most Muslims live in West and North Africa, where the strain of HIV is considered less virulent, and that virginity is very important in the Muslim religion.

In addition, while Muslims often practice polygamy, they tend not to have other partners besides their wives, so the chances of introducing the virus are lower than with men who have many casual partners.

In Uganda, the rate of infection dropped pri-

> **HIV/AIDS may not be curable, but it is certainly preventable and treatable."**
>
> WHO
> World Health Report 2004

marily because abstinence and faithfulness were encouraged, and Christian churches were on the frontline of this movement. While Christian churches have been promoting abstinence and faithfulness, so far no research has been able to indicate that church-going Christians have HIV/AIDS rates that differ from the general population. Churches have been at the forefront of caring for people with AIDS and organizing orphan care and support. But some experts believe that the church could have been a more important factor in prevention, citing the hesitancy of Christians in Africa to discuss sex and some of the early teachings that HIV infections only resulted from "sinful" behavior.

Increasingly, leaders of all religions are speaking out about HIV/AIDS to promote responsible preventive behavior, encouraging testing, reduce stigma, and mobilize care and support for those affected.

How is HIV/AIDS spread in different parts of the world?

■ The growing AIDS crisis in Eastern Europe and the former Soviet countries is primarily due to IV drug usage, especially among young people who are sexually active. Some reports say that heroin is now cheaper than alcohol, but needles are still expensive and are routinely reused.

IV drug usage is also growing in China, where HIV infections were spread originally by unsafe blood-collection practices. Prostitutes spread the infection in some Asian countries, but Vietnam's rising number of infections are primarily attributed to IV drug usage.

In Latin America and the Caribbean, both IV drug usage and homosexual transmission account for most of the primary infections.

In most countries, HIV/AIDS usually begins as

FACT:

Brazil was the first developing country to have implemented a universal antiretroviral distribution program.

a narrowly concentrated epidemic contained within "high-risk groups" such as intravenous drug users, prostitutes, and homosexual men. Evidence has revealed that under certain circumstances, HIV will eventually enter the general population through heterosexual sex. Once the prevalence of infection reaches a certain level—about 1 percent—it will spread rapidly to the general population through heterosexual activity.

What about AIDS in developed countries? Isn't the rate going down?

■ UNAIDS estimates that there are 1.6 million people living with AIDS in relatively high income countries. The rate may be rising, in part because more people are living longer due to ARV drugs. While 64,000 new cases were reported in 2003, only 22,000 deaths from AIDS were reported, a declining number. However, there is concern that a growing percentage of those infected do not know it because they have not been tested. In the US, estimates are that as many as one quarter of the infected do not know they are HIV positive.

What groups of people in developed countries are contracting HIV?

■ Sex between men continues to be the most common way to be infected in the US, as well as Australia, Canada, and several European countries. In the US, the African-American community now accounts for almost half of all new infections and is the leading cause of death for African-American women aged 25–34, according to UNAIDS. Many of these women were infected through partners who were IV drug users.

> **African countries face a stark choice. If they do not find ways to care for the growing multitude of AIDS orphans, they could soon find their streets crowded with angry, intoxicated adolescents. Besides being a human tragedy, this could aggravate the continent's already high levels of crime."**
>
> **Emma Guest**
> **In *Children of AIDS***
> **(Pluto Press, 2001)**

What are the Millennium Development Goals and what do they have to do with most Americans?

■ The Millennium Development Goals (MDG) were adopted by the UN in 2000 as goals that every country could hope to achieve by 2015. They provide a framework in which national goals can be set and in which the international community can agree on priorities. The US as a country, and most humanitarian and religious groups in the developed world, support these as basic rights and expectations for citizens of any country. They are aimed at closing some of the gap between the "haves" and "have nots" of the world and are meant to help poorer countries begin to set sound policies.

Millennium Development Goals

1. **Eradicate extreme poverty and hunger.**

2. **Achieve universal primary education.**

3. **Promote gender equality and empower women.**

4. **Reduce child mortality.**

5. **Improve maternal health.**

6. **Combat HIV/AIDS, malaria, and other diseases.**

7. **Ensure environmental sustainability.**

8. **Develop a global partnership for development.**

FACT:

Almost 6 million people now need anti-retroviral drugs but only about 400,000 received them in 2003.

Activists march through Bangkok campaigning for safe sex and condom use.

LAWS AND POLITICS

The politics of AIDS are as complex as the political systems around the world. So, too, are the laws concerning the disease.

Is it illegal to discriminate against people with AIDS?

■ For the most part, it is illegal to discriminate against anyone who is HIV positive or has AIDS in the US and in other developed countries. Americans with AIDS are protected under some provisions of the Americans with Disabilities Act (ADA). Because it is now understood that HIV cannot be contracted through casual contact, children who are HIV positive are less likely to be stigmatized by school systems. If their conditions are known, the issue should be considered confidential. Of course, this may not be how it works in practice, and American society must continue to fight this prejudice.

In many countries, people who are HIV positive have ARV treatments covered by national health insurance. This has led some patients to move to countries where such treatment is provided free of charge.

However, people with HIV/AIDS in many parts of the world are not similarly protected. Many developing countries have no laws protecting people from discrimination. And even where laws exist, society continues to stigmatize those with AIDS. This contributes to a lack of interest in testing and means that people will remain in denial about their condition and may continue to infect others.

In some parts of the world, patients who appear to have AIDS are not welcomed in hospitals and women who are HIV positive may find it difficult to have their babies delivered in a hospital. In Eastern Europe and the former Soviet bloc countries, where

Five Reasons
for Optimism

Despite all the bad news about HIV/AIDS, there are some reasons to be hopeful.

Some countries have begun to reduce the rate of HIV infections.

1. According to the UNAIDS 2004 report, Brazil, the Dominican Republic, Uganda, and Thailand have all reported reductions in their rate of HIV infections.

Progress is being made on mother-to-child transmission.

2. It was once believed that an HIV positive mother would always give birth to an infected baby. It is now known that this is not true and there are ways to reduce the chance of infection, as well as ways to use drug therapies to further reduce the risk of transfer. (See page 15.)

Private and public partnerships are becoming more common.

3. In the face of such an overwhelming crisis, self-interests are giving way to cooperation in an unparalleled manner. This could pave the way for more partnerships to address other world problems in the future.

People in wealthy countries are learning more about the developing world.

4. The focus on AIDS has also helped bring attention to other complications of poverty, such as poor health systems, lack of communication, and underdeveloped governments.

Cultural prejudices are being challenged in developing countries.

5. Education about AIDS prevention is also encouraging discussions about the role of women, exposing misconceptions about sexual practices and helping dispel myths about traditional healers. Because of the urgency and consequences, progress is being made within years, not within generations.

HIV infections are spreading rapidly because of IV drug use, the hospitals are struggling to develop appropriate procedures to deal with patients who are infected without further stigmatizing them.

Can a person who is HIV positive immigrate to the US?

■ Officially, the US Immigration service can deny entry to a person with a communicable disease of public health significance. The list of diseases that qualify includes HIV/AIDS. However, people who seek temporary entry into the US are not routinely tested, although if they apply for a visa they must declare themselves to be free of disease. This declaration does not have to be proven by testing, and immigration officers can only call for a test if there is suspicion of disease. Many millions of other visitors enter the US without a visa and do not have to make a declaration of their status.

Refugees and those seeking asylum in the US

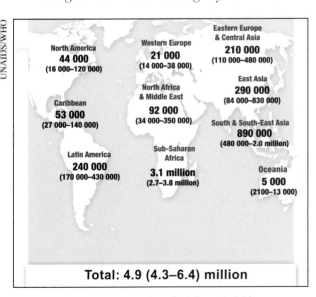

North America
44 000
(16 000–120 000)

Western Europe
21 000
(14 000–38 000)

Eastern Europe & Central Asia
210 000
(110 000–480 000)

North Africa & Middle East
92 000
(34 000–350 000)

East Asia
290 000
(84 000–830 000)

Caribbean
53 000
(27 000–140 000)

South & South-East Asia
890 000
(480 000–2.0 million)

Latin America
240 000
(170 000–430 000)

Sub-Saharan Africa
3.1 million
(2.7–3.8 million)

Oceania
5 000
(2100–13 000)

Total: 4.9 (4.3–6.4) million

Estimated Number of Adults and Children Newly Infected with HIV during 2004

can apply for a waiver even if they have tested HIV positive. People can apply for asylum in the US on the basis of persecution in their country because of their HIV status. An HIV test is required for those seeking refugee status but not for those seeking asylum. But if an asylum seeker wants to apply for permanent residence in the US, a test is required.

The US policy has been widely criticized by public health advocates who feel it is inconsistent and encourages those who might be HIV positive to either avoid testing or hide their status. It also officially stigmatizes those with HIV and does not meet the World Health Organization guidelines for testing. And since many millions of people can enter the US without even declaring their status and millions more are never tested, there is a good probability that many HIV positive people enter the US daily from other countries.

The average American doesn't use IV drugs and is not sexually promiscuous. Doesn't that mean we are not personally vulnerable to being infected?

■ Public health officials agree that HIV infections are entirely preventable. While the disease is considered "communicable" because it can pass from one person to another, it is only contagious when a person engages in specific activities and comes in contact with the virus. The disease does not flow freely among a population. HIV cannot survive for long outside the body and is easily killed by sterilization.

The blood supply in the US is regularly tested, so the chance of infection from a transfusion is considered remote. Dentists and doctors sterilize their equipment, and disposable syringes have become the norm to prevent even accidental usage on more than one patient.

However, there are other public health risks associated with HIV that may be more of a threat to the general population. Tuberculosis is becoming far more common because those with suppressed immune systems acquire it more readily. The incidence of tuberculosis worldwide is growing rapidly and can become a major public health factor even for people who are not infected with HIV. People with depressed immune systems are easily infected with highly communicable diseases and may then become carriers of that disease.

Why do some people advocate legalizing prostitution to help fight AIDS?

■ Prostitution is already legal in many countries. It is even legal in parts of Nevada. There is a growing debate internationally over whether it is better to recognize that the sex trade exists and therefore regulate and protect sex workers from becoming infected or spreading HIV infections. Other groups believe that any such tendency only encourages an immoral practice. Some governments, such as Thailand, have continued to officially ban prostitution but have "unofficially" provided education, testing, and protection about HIV to commercial sex workers (sometimes referred to as CSWs). Some organizations feel that a person has the right to choose to become a sex worker. Other groups consider any transactional sex to be a fundamental violation of the dignity of a person and an immoral act.

In some poor countries, children are enticed into the sex trade by being lured from the country to the city with promises of jobs. Because of the growing understanding that many prostitutes are infected with AIDS, a higher price is paid for virgins in brothels. Sadly, this means that younger and younger children are being coerced or forced into prostitution.

FACT:

A severe shortage of health workers exists in many developing countries, potentially limiting treatment and testing facilities even if funding and drugs are available.

Although no one officially endorses such practices, those who favor legalization of prostitution sometimes argue that recognition and regulation of brothels would help eliminate the abuses of children. This is, of course, another controversial position.

What is sex tourism?

■ People who travel from their own country to another country with the purpose of engaging in commercial sex are called sex tourists. Many are seeking young prostitutes, especially children, because they are believed to be less likely to be HIV infected. Such activity is known as child sex tourism (CST). This practice is illegal in most countries, but may not be enforced. Asian countries such as Thailand and Cambodia have been known as destinations for sex tourists from the US.

What is TIP?

■ TIP stands for Trafficking in Persons and is used most often in reference to an office in the US Department of State that tracks and tries to prevent practices that exploit people for sex, labor, slavery, servitude, or organ removal. The US government strongly opposes legalized prostitution and believes that in countries where prostitution is legalized there is still a black market in illegal sex activity, often including trafficking victims. The TIP office has launched a campaign to educate Americans about the illegality of child sex tourism.

Why don't women have legal rights in many developing countries?

■ Some countries have obviously discriminatory laws preventing women from owning property, voting, and enjoying other rights we might consid-

> **We agree to use the challenge presented by the HIV/AIDS epidemic as an opportunity for spiritual growth, to care for one another, to support the living and the dying, and to appreciate the gift of life."**
>
> From *The South Asian Inter-Faith Pledge on Children, Young People and HIV/AIDS, 2003*

er basic. Other countries do not necessarily have laws that hurt women, but the practice of discrimination is widespread and abused women have no recourse. In some countries, women are banned from schools after a certain age, educational resources are limited, and boys are felt to deserve schooling more than girls. Marriage laws often allow girls to be married at a very young age, which further hurts their chances of pursuing an education or any form of independence.

What are inheritance laws?

■ In many countries, women are not allowed to own land, so if a woman's husband dies, she is either thrown off the land or the land passes to a relative of her husband's. She must marry him, become part of his family, or lose her land and possibly her children.

Because developing countries are often heavily agrarian, the land is an important family asset.

HIV infection increases both the incidence and severity of clinical malaria in adults.

Ted Haddock/International Justice Missions

Young prostitutes anxiously wait as police raid their brothel in South Asia. Sex trafficking and commercial sexual exploitation of women and girls is a massive engine in the spread of AIDS.

When a father is designating his land for inheritance, he leaves the land only to his sons. But in some places, progressive fathers are beginning to leave land to their daughters as well.

Why won't more leaders take the initiative to stop the spread of AIDS like President Museveni did in Uganda?

■ Admitting that problems exist has never been a popular move for politicians or government leaders. While President Museveni is widely praised now, in the early days of declaring war on AIDS he was not all that popular. By drawing attention to the problem, he created a great deal of discomfort in Ugandan society, where talk about sex was not common and men did not feel they needed to be accountable for their sexual practices. Because of the openness about the problem in Uganda, many citizens found that they were stigmatized when traveling out of the country and in some cases were even barred from entering certain countries. AIDS is an expensive issue to address and does not result in visible results such as roads or schools.

Still, other countries have taken steps to curb the spread of infection or provide education, prevention, and treatment. Senegal was actually one of the first countries to help stop the spread of the disease by using a public campaign and enlisting Muslim clerics to help stop behaviors that might contribute to the spread of infection. Thailand's government became very aggressive about educating sex workers and promoting the use of condoms. Brazil has also been on the forefront of stopping the spread of HIV infections and providing free treatment to those infected. Many countries are becoming more forthright about the problem as they recognize that funds are available to help them fight the disease.

> **It is easy to despair of AIDS. But let us bear in mind the many formidable challenges that Africa has already faced and overcome: wars of independence, global economic upheaval, droughts, floods. Then let us remember that unlike any of these, AIDS is completely preventable.**
>
> *Intensifying Action Against HIV/AIDS in Africa*
> **World Bank, 1999**

Is it true that there is mandatory AIDS testing in Cuba and those who are infected are imprisoned?

■ Cuba was exposed relatively early to AIDS because soldiers from Uganda went there to train. In the early 1980s, Fidel Castro began to reject soldiers who carried a mysterious disease.

While Castro has been widely criticized for such practices as mandatory testing and other human rights violations, some have suggested that there may be something to learn from a country that suffers from widespread poverty but has managed to contain the HIV infection rate, unlike Haiti, where the rate of infection is growing rapidly.

In fact, many now suggest that the Cuban example may be helpful to other developing countries. Widespread education helps all Cubans understand how to prevent AIDS, those who are HIV positive are given access to free drugs and training on preventing transmission, and the country is conducting extensive research. While those who test positive are placed in sanitariums, this is now done as part of a course of treatment and to help educate them on prevention methods.

Why is there so much discussion about international laws and agreements in regard to AIDS?

■ While each country must deal with HIV/AIDS by developing policies and enacting appropriate laws, the crisis is truly international and can only be effectively addressed on an international basis.

Human rights policies are largely driven by the UN. Trade agreements are subject to WTO

FACT:

In Viet Nam, more than 20 percent of injecting drug users are believed to be HIV positive.

policies. In many ways, the HIV/AIDS crisis will force nations to decide if they are willing and able to cooperate internationally. The US has held back from supporting many of the key international strategies to fight AIDS and is becoming increasingly divided from other countries on the issues.

What is meant by advocacy and what role does it play?

■ Advocacy simply means to give a voice to a cause or to people who have no voice. In the US, advocacy on behalf of AIDS was led by entertainers, such as Elizabeth Taylor, who raised millions of dollars to help fight the disease and discrimination against those infected. Advocacy is primarily used to influence public opinion and policies. Bono is one of the leading advocates on behalf of those affected by AIDS in Africa.

Many humanitarian organizations have led advocacy campaigns to increase funding for international AIDS prevention and treatment. Advocacy will be increasingly important if wealthy countries are going to continue to contribute to the needs of developing countries.

> **"When there's conflict, drought, famine, major population movement, or major military movement, you can suspect that HIV/AIDS is running wild."**
>
> **Kristin Kalla,**
> **Director**
> **CORE Initiative**

I'm not a tourist attraction.
It's a crime to make me one.

Stop child sex tourism.

World Vision

U.S. Immigration and Customs Enforcement

World Vision's program to combat child sex tourism uses billboards such as this to deter abusers.

Major Challenges
in Fighting AIDS

HIV/AIDS has been officially recognized as a unique disease for twenty years. According to UNAIDS, the greatest challenges facing those who are responding to the crisis today are:

- Dealing with the high number of infected women.

- Dealing with the growing numbers of infected young people.

- Scaling up treatment programs.

- Delivering health services.

- Scaling up prevention programs.

- Tackling stigma and discrimination.

- Caring for orphans.

Quilts representing American AIDS deaths stretch out before the Capitol Building.

WHAT CAN BE DONE?

Learning the facts about the AIDS pandemic is the first step. But how can anyone really make a difference? Here are some thoughts.

I'm just one person. How can I possibly do anything that will change the situation?

■ There's a saying in Uganda: "One plus one soon makes a bundle." When Ugandans were dealing with an HIV infection rate that threatened to wipe out a considerable portion of their population, they learned the importance of each person doing something to change the situation. So, too, each of us can dedicate ourselves to doing something to make a difference.

The first thing we can do is become educated. Reading this book is part of doing that. Sharing it with someone else is another step. Reading the books listed in the bibliography or contacting the websites listed are also important steps. Sign up for a daily Google news alert on AIDS. If you do you'll notice that AIDS is covered less by American newspapers than the press in other countries. That might move you to write a letter to the editor of your local newspaper suggesting that covering the AIDS pandemic is important.

Writing to your member of Congress or other officials to encourage AIDS funding is also an important step toward making sure that those in public office know that their constituents care about the pandemic.

Three websites that can also help you think creatively are www.apathyislethal.com, wwwdata.org, and www.compassion.com. All three contain stories of how individuals have made a difference and offer resources for helping raise awareness and funds.

Funding is crucial to prevent and treat HIV/AIDS. So far individuals have not given very enthusiastically to the cause. Giving to a charity

Argentina, Barbados, Brazil, Chile, Costa Rica, Cuba, Mexico, and Uruguay all offer universal coverage for anti-retroviral treatments.

involved in AIDS is an important step to take, even if it's only a small gift.

How do I decide which charity to support?

■ You might start by deciding if there is some area of the crisis that is especially of interest to you. Are you interested in educating people about HIV and helping prevent its spread? Do you feel a special desire to help AIDS orphans? Do you feel an affinity toward a particular country?

Some organizations are especially involved in prevention while others deal primarily with treatment. Some are focused on the needs of women, and some work exclusively with children.

Some organizations spend much of their time advocating for causes related to AIDS such as legal rights for women. Some are dedicated to making drug treatments available for a wide number of people.

Many faith-based organizations are involved in various aspects of HIV/AIDS work, so you might want to support an organization that is consistent with your background and upholds your beliefs. You might also check to see if your denomination or faith has a related medical mission.

Will I be able to volunteer to get involved directly?

■ There are many opportunities to get involved with fundraising, administrative work, and AIDS education in this country. But opportunities to go overseas are generally limited to people with some medical training or other professional background.

Individuals with nursing degrees and medical training are desperately needed to work in developing countries. Doctors Without Borders is one of the most well known organizations sending medical staff overseas, but there are a variety of medical missions looking for individuals to work.

"For me, as an HIV positive person, this is the time to show that the church is not a mausoleum for saints, but a place of hope for the sick."
Rev. Christo Greyling
Africa HIV/AIDS Church Relations Advisor, World Vision

How can I get my congregation involved?

■ Congregations, service clubs, schools, and other groups all have the potential to raise awareness and significant funds for fighting HIV/AIDS.

You might start by asking if it is possible to start a task force or to offer a class on HIV/AIDS. There are materials available from denominations as well as through www.data.org. You could also put together a fundraiser for HIV/AIDS and use it as an opportunity to bring a speaker in to talk about the situation.

If your congregation is interested in becoming involved in advocacy, Bread for the World has a program called an "offering of letters" in which congregations are asked to write letters to members of Congress and other public officials. You can find information at www.breadfortheworld.org. Other organizations also sponsor advocacy campaigns and will provide free materials for your group.

You might also consider ordering some of the free materials available from UNAIDS, WHO, the CDC, and many of the humanitarian organizations and placing them in your church or school library.

How do I know what data to trust?

■ As stated previously, most of the statistics quoted on HIV/AIDS are estimates and even those are revised regularly. Most organizations consider UNAIDS and WHO as the official sources of information and that is why they are used for most of the data in this book. You can go to the websites at www.unaids.org or www.who.org to find statistics, free publications, and much more information. For statistics in the US, the CDC is the best source at www.cdc.gov. The National Institutes of Health also has information at www.nih.gov.

FACT:

The estimated number of pediatric AIDS cases in the US fell from 952 in 1992 to 92 in 2002.

Selected Bibliography

■ *2004 Report on the Global AIDS epidemic.* UNAIDS, 2004.

■ *African Development Indicators-2004.* World Bank Africa Database. The World Bank, 2004.

■ *The AIDS Dictionary.* Sarah Barbara Watstein. Facts on File, 1998.

■ *AIDS Epidemic Update, December 2003.* UNAIDS, 2004.

■ *The AIDS Pandemic.* Lawrence O. Gostin. University of North Carolina Press, 2004.

■ *AIDS in the Twenty-First Century.* Tony Barnett and Alan Whiteside. Palgrave, 2002.

■ *The AWAKE Project.* Compiled by Jenny Eaton and Kate Etue. W Publishing, 2002.

■ *Black Death.* Susan Hunter. Palgrave, 2003.

■ *Breaking the Conspiracy of Silence.* Donald E. Messer. Fortress Press, 2004.

■ *Children of AIDS.* Emma Guest. Pluto Press, 2001.

■ *Global AIDS: Myths and Facts.* Alexander Irwin, Joyce Millen, and Dorothy Fallows. South End Press, 2003.

■ *Glossary of HIV/AIDS-Related Terms.* Treatment Information Service, CDC. Department of Health and Human Services, 2004.

■ *Intensifying Action Against HIV/AIDS in Africa.* Africa Region/The World Bank. The World Bank, 2000.

■ *HIV/AIDS—The Faith Community Responds.* Pamela Potter, Editor. Georgetown University Press, 2004.

■ *HIV/AIDS in Africa.* Edited by Ezekiel Kalipeni, Susan Craddock, Joseph R. Oppong, and Jayati Ghosh. Blackwell, 2004.

■ *HIV/AIDS Prevention and Education.* Ken Casey, Executive Editor. World Vision, 2003.

■ *HIV/AIDS Surveillance Report.* Public Health Service, CDC. Department of Health and Human Services, 2002.

■ *The Invisible People.* Greg Behrman. Free Press, 2004.

■ *Mini-Atlas of Global Development.* The World Bank, 2004.

■ *Moving Mountains, The Race to Treat Global AIDS.* Anne-Christine D'Adesky. Verso, 2004.

■ *The No-Nonsense Guide to HIV/AIDS.* Shereen Usdin. Verso, 2003.

■ *Pocket World in Figures.* The Economist editors. Profile Books, 2003.

■ *Rethinking AIDS Prevention.* Edward C. Green. Praeger, 2003.

■ "Scaling Up Care and Treatment for People Living with HIV/AIDS in the Developing World." Ira Magaziner. *World Affairs,* Summer/Fall 2004, p 27.

■ *Trafficking in Persons Report.* Staff of US Department of State, Office to Monitor and Combat Trafficking in Persons. US Department of State Publications, 2004.

■ "Who Is AIDS?" Kate Wilkinson. University of Connecticut Dissertation, 2004.

■ *The World Health Report 2004.* World Health Organization, 2004.

Websites Used Extensively

■ www.AllAfrica.com

■ www.ApathyIsLethal.org

■ www.AVERT.org

■ www.BBC.com

■ www.CARE.org

■ www.CDC.gov

■ www.DATA.org

■ www.NIH.gov

■ www.UNAIDS.org

■ www.UNICEF.org

■ www.WHO.org

■ www.WorldBank.org

■ www.WorldVision.org